AutoCAD LT Companion

About the author

Jeff Roberts B.Sc., M.Sc., PGD has used AutoCAD since the
early 1980s in his former profession as a land and building
surveyor, and has used AutoCAD LT since its release. He has
been manager of the AutoDesk authorised training centre at Neath
College since 1988 and is an AutoDesk authorised developer. He
has also acted as a consultant to industry on CAD strategies and
on multimedia development.

AUTOCAD LT

A COMPANION GUIDE

J.T. Roberts

INTERNATIONAL

THOMSON
PUBLISHING

Autodesk

Press

I(T)P® An International Thomson Publishing Company

London • Bonn • Boston • Johannesburg • Madrid • Melbourne • Mexico City • New York • Paris
Singapore • Tokyo • Toronto • Albany NY • Belmont CA • Cincinnati OH • Detroit MI

Autodesk Trademarks

The following trademarks are registered in the U.S. Patent and Trademark Office by Autodesk, Inc.: ADI, ATC, Autodesk, the Autodesk logo, Autodesk Renderman, AutoCAD, AutoCAD Training Center, AutoLISP, AutoShade, AutoSketch, AutoSolid, and Generic CADD.

The following are trademarks of Autodesk, Inc.: ACAD, Advanced Modeling Extension, Advance User Interface, AME, AUI, AutoCAD Development System, Autodesk Animator, Autodesk Animator Clips, Autodesk Animator Theatre, Autodesk AutoFlix, CA Lab, DXF, and James Gleick's CHAOS: The Software.

Third Party Trademarks

Renderman is registered trademark of Pixar used by Autodesk under license from Pixar.

All other brand and product names are trademarks or registered trademarks of their respective companies.

Copyright © 1997 Autodesk, Inc.
Published by Autodesk Press, a division of International Thomson Publishing.
I⑪P The ITP logo is a trademark under license.

For more information contact:

Autodesk Press
3 Columbia Circle, Box 15-015
Albany, New York, USA 12212-5015

International Thomson Editores
Campos Eliseos 385, Piso 7
Colonia Polanco
1560 Mexico D.F.

Autodesk Press
International Thomson Publishing Europe
Berkshire House
168–173 High Holborn
London WC1V 7AA

International Thomson Publishing GmbH
Königswinterer Strasse 418
53227 Bonn, Germany

Thomas Nelson Australia
102 Dodds Steet
South Melbourne, Victoria 3205
Australia

International Thomson Publishing France
1, rue St. Georges
75009 Paris, France

Nelson Canada
11290 Birchmont Road
Scarborough, Ontario
Canada, M1K 5G4

International Thomson Publishing Japan
Hirakawacho Kyowa Building, 3f
2-2-1 Hirakawa-cho Chiyoda-ku
Tokyo 102, Japan

International Thomson Publishing Southern Africa
Building 18, Constantia Park
240 Old Pretoria Road
P.O. Box 2459
Halfway House, 1685 South Africa

Typeset by Hodgson Williams Associates, Tunbridge Wells and Cambridge

Printed in Great Britain by Clays Ltd, Bungay, Suffolk

ISBN 1-85032-341-0 (Student Edition)

ISBN 1-85032-340-2 (Companion Edition)

DEDICATION

For my son, Andrew,
in recognition of our
continuing love and friendship

ACKNOWLEDGEMENTS

I would like to thank the dependable Robin Wilson of Autodesk Press, and the publishing production team for advice and expert guidance on publishing this product.

Contents

1 Getting Started

MS-DOS Windows

If you have a PC with MS-DOS Windows version 3.1 or higher your screen will look similar to the one shown in Figure 1.1. You will not have the same program icons or windows but after loading AutoCAD LT you should have an icon named as AutoCAD LT. You may wish to add the version number to be more precise.

If you have Windows 95 your screen will look similar to that shown in Figure 1.2. The program is activated by clicking once on the AutoCAD LT name.

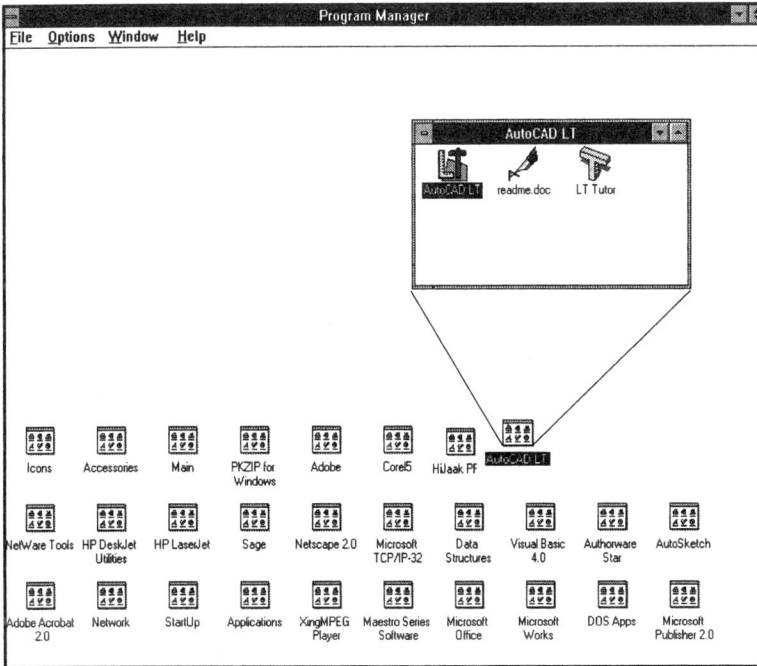

Figure 1.1 The Windows 3.1 Program Manager showing standard Windows 3.1 icons along with the AutoCAD LT program icon.

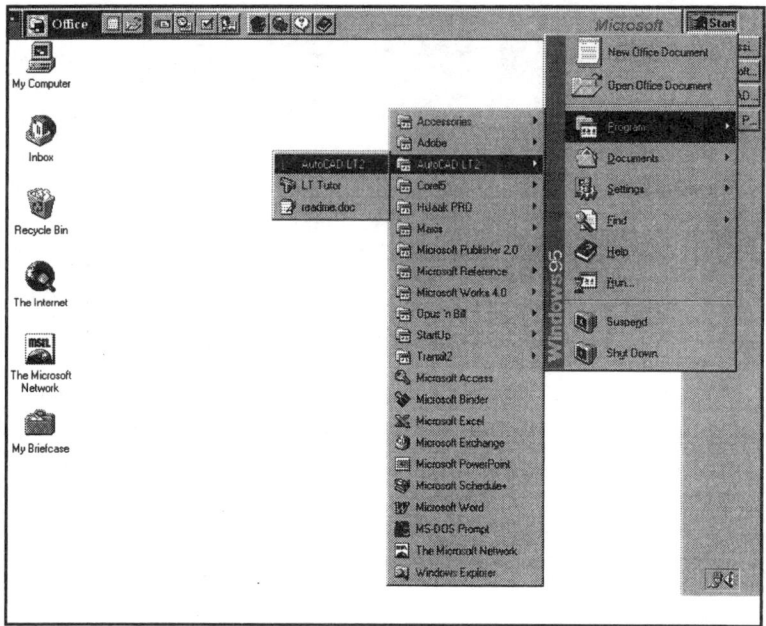

Figure 1.2   A Windows 95 Graphical User Interface (GUI).

Starting AutoCAD LT

When you activate AutoCAD LT the Windows interface is replaced by the initial LT window showing the ownership and licensing details as shown in Figure 1.3.

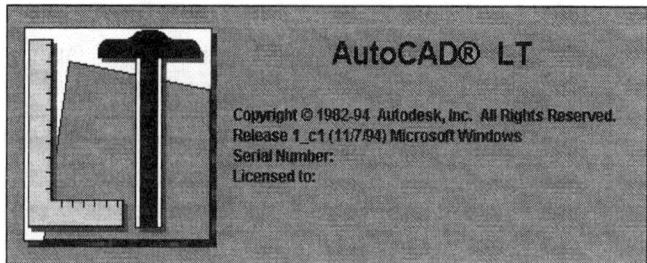

Figure 1.3   The initial AutoCAD LT window.

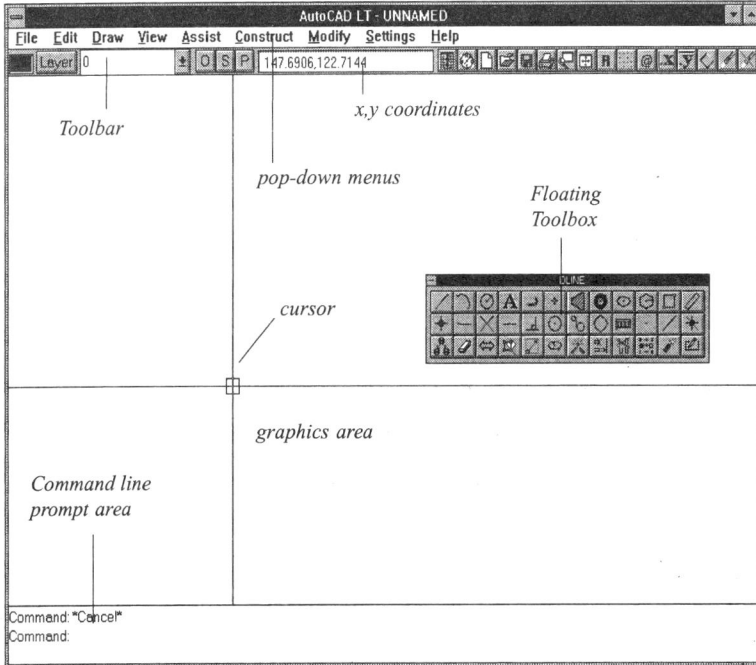

Figure 1.4   The AutoCAD LT graphics window.

This is quickly followed by the AutoCAD LT graphics window. This window contains many of the drawing, editing and construction tools that you will use regularly in your drawing sessions. Figure 1.4 shows the screen at a resolution of 800×600 pixels (Extended VGA, commonly and incorrectly called Super VGA). Lower resolutions than this do not display all of the tools in the Toolbar and yours may not include the Cancel and blank buttons.

Before moving on, get used to the various features of the graphics window by using your mouse. Note how the mouse is in the form of crosshairs in the graphics window but changes to the usual arrow pointer when it is moved outside the graphics window. Note also how the coordinate values change, in the coordinate display, as you move the mouse. These numbers record the exact location of the centre of the crosshair on the screen at any time.

Move the mouse over the Menu Bar and activate the pull-down menus. Click anywhere outside the pull-down menus in the graphics area to 'roll up' each of them.

The Toolbar

If you have used Windows applications previously, the New, Open, Save and Print icons will be familiar to you. AutoCAD LT also provides two icons for undoing and redoing actions along with the facility to enlarge a view of the drawing by using the Zoom button. The question mark provides detailed online help as shown in Figure 1.5.

When the mouse pointer is positioned over any of the buttons in the Toolbar an explanatory rectangular bubble appears describing the function of that icon.

Figure 1.5   The Toolbar.

The Ortho, Snap and Mspace buttons can be 'toggled' on or off with the left mouse button, and will look as if they are 'depressed' when activated as shown in Figure 1.6.

Figure 1.6   Snap is set on.

To help you locate your position in the drawing, x, y coordinates are shown on the screen and they change as the cursor is moved around the screen as shown in Figure 1.7. How to draw by specifying exact measurements is covered in detail in Chapter 3.

Figure 1.7   The coordinate display.

Layering a drawing (as in the manual drafting process of using over-lays) is advisable as you can group various types of objects. One way of activating the Layer Control dialogue box is by clicking on the overlaid sheets in the Toolbar as shown in Figure 1.8. A list of layers is shown by the down arrow and changing colours via the colour icon. Creating layers is discussed more fully in Chapter 3.

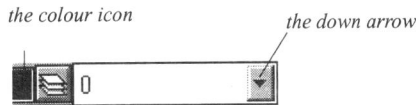

Figure 1.8 The Layer Control box.

The remaining icons on the Toolbar govern the location and visibility of the floating Toolbox, the aerial view, and the button to cancel an activity. The empty buttons are available for customizing as shown in Figure 1.9.

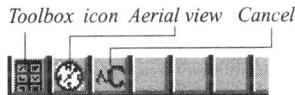

Figure 1.9 The Toolbox, Aerial view and Cancel buttons.

The Toolbox

The Toolbox can be repositioned by clicking in the narrow band above the icons, holding the mouse button down and dragging to a desired position. This feature is particularly useful when drawing is in progress.

The Toolbox icon in the Toolbar governs the positioning and visibility of the Toolbox. It is a window containing icons that initiate commands and is shown in Figure 1.10.

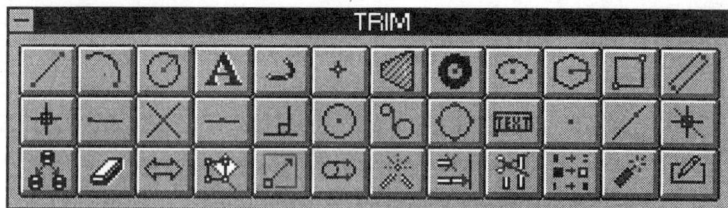

Figure 1.10   The Toolbox.

The Graphics Area

The graphics area is where you will produce your drawing. The drawing boundaries can be changed to any size and your screen will be similar to that shown on page 3 before any drawing is commenced. You will see your cursor move around this area as the mouse is moved. You will also see the cursor change to a pointer depending on the activity.

Command Line Prompt Area

The Command line is where commands are entered through the keyboard and where you respond to prompts and information. Above the command line there are two lines of previous prompts called the command history. If you need to view more previous history, you can use the F2 function key to switch to the inbuilt text window.

The Text Window

This window contains a complete history of the current drawing session. It can be used to view long outputs such as those produced by the List command. Forward and backward movement through the history is achieved by using the scroll arrows as shown in Figure 1.11. If you press F2 while in the text window it will return you to the graphics screen. If either the text window or the graphics screen has been minimized, pressing the F2 key will restore it to its full size.

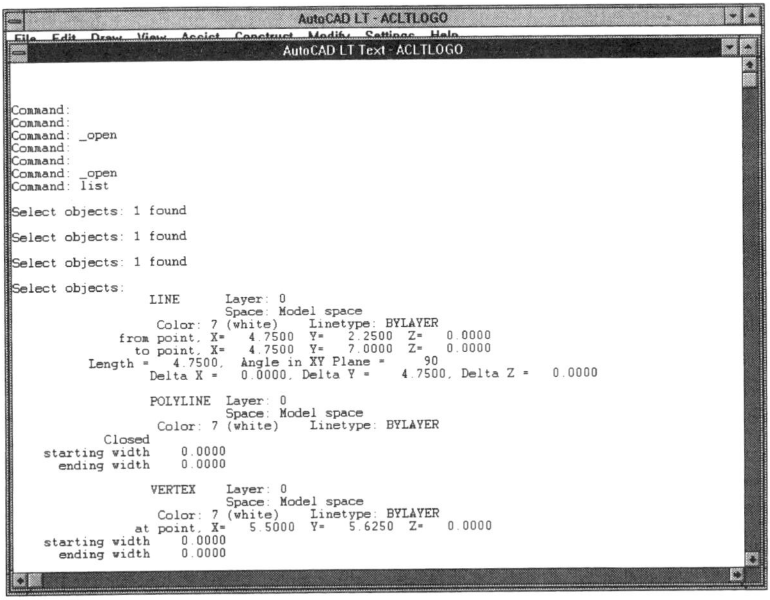

Figure 1.11 The AutoCAD LT text window.

The Function Keys

The Function keys or 'F' keys are located on your keyboard directly above the alphanumeric keys as shown in Figure 1.12. AutoCAD LT uses these keys for special purposes or functions.

F1   Opens AutoCAD LT Help

F2   Toggles between graphics screen and text screen

F3   Not used

F4   Not used

F5   Alternates between isometric drawing planes

F6   Turns the coordinate display On or Off

keys F1-F12

Figure 1.12   The AutoCAD LT function keys.

F7	Turns grid On or Off
F8	Turns Ortho On or Off
F9	Turns Snap On or Off
F10	Opens the File Menu
F11	Not used
F12	Not used

Other keys used for special functions are:

Ctrl+C	Cancels the current command
@	Indicates the last specified point
<	Indicates that the following number is an angle

The Pointing Device

The pointing device is more commonly known as the mouse and may have two or three buttons. The left button is used for picking points in the graphics area, commands in the border surrounding the graphics area and in the Toolbox if it is visible. The right button is the equivalent of the Enter key on the keyboard and completes an activity.

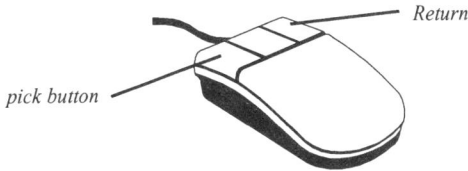

Return

pick button

Figure 1.13   A typical three-button mouse.

Arranging the Program Groups

After application software is loaded through Windows 3.1, the desktop is changed as shown in Figure 1.14. The applications or program groups are shown in a 'tiled' display which is activated through the *Window/Tile* menu.

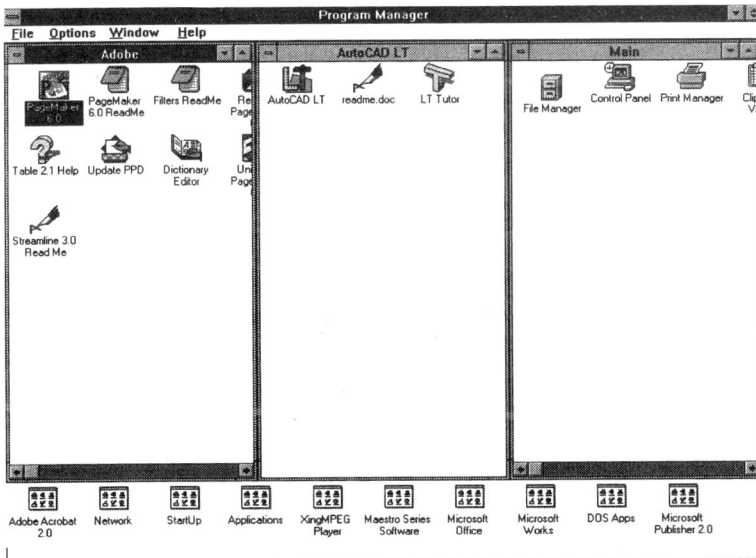

Figure 1.14   Tiled program groups.

In this pull-down you also have the option of 'cascading' the application windows as shown in Figure 1.15.

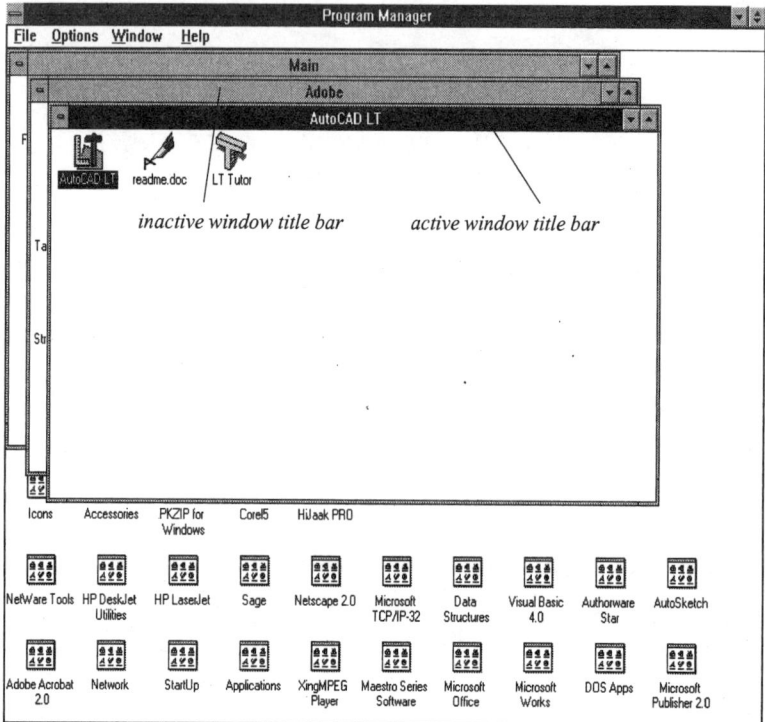

Figure 1.15   Cascaded program groups.

Resizing Windows

Windows can be resized by moving the pointer to any edge or corner of the active window. At the edge it will change to a double-headed arrow, and by holding down the pointer button on the mouse the window can be 'dragged' to its new size as shown in Figure 1.16. Practise changing the size of the active window.

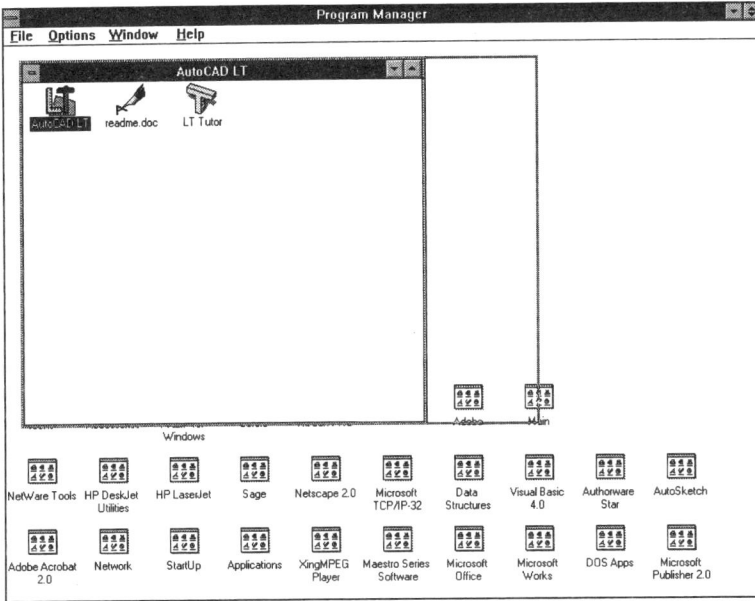

Figure 1.16 Resizing a window.

Using File Manager

The File Manager is a program that lets you copy, move and generally organize files on your hard or floppy disk. It performs DOS commands like Copy, Diskcopy, Format, MkDir, RmDir and Ren. Also, it allows you to view several drives and directories at once.

To start File Manager, double-click on the File Manager icon which is found in the Main program group. The File Manager window contains another window, divided into two. The left half shows the directory tree structure of the current drive. The right half shows a list of files in the current directory. You will recognize which is the current directory by the open folder icon in the left half of the window. To view files in any directory, click on a directory icon in the left window and you will see the right window display the files in that directory as shown in Figure 1.17.

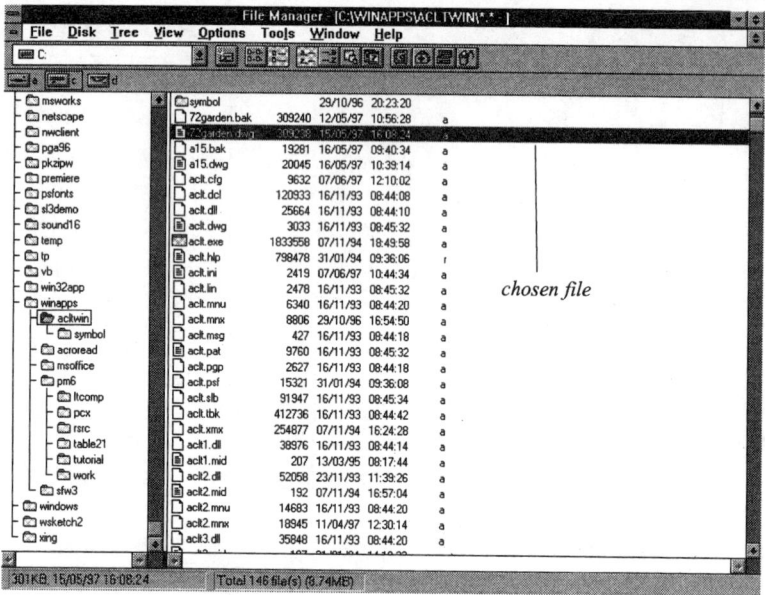

Figure 1.17   Using File Manager.

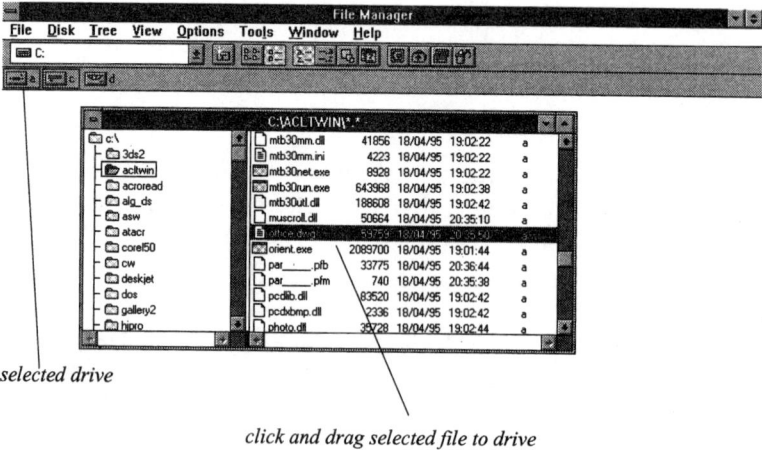

Figure 1.18   Copying a saved drawing file to floppy disk.

Copying Files to Disk

To copy a saved drawing file to disk, open the *Main* program icon and double-click on File Manager. Locate the file by scrolling through the directories on the left-hand side. In our example we have located the *Office* drawing called *Office.dwg*. Click on the file name icon on the right-hand side and, holding the button down, drag the pointer over to the drive name located at the top left-hand corner as shown in Figure 1.18. The file icon will appear to be connected to the pointer. A warning dialogue box will appear as shown in Figure 1.19. Click on *Yes* and it is replaced with a message window telling you that it is copying to the selected drive. The message window will contain the file size also.

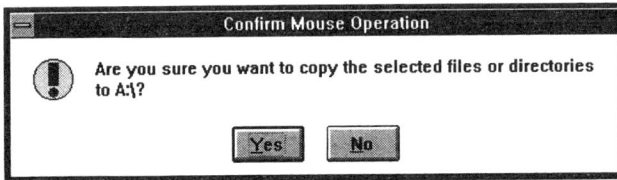

Figure 1.19 Windows Confirmation dialogue box.

2 Drawing Setup

Initial Setup

After you have double-clicked on the AutoCAD LT icon the AutoCAD LT logo and licensing information will appear as shown on page 2. This is followed by the window shown in Figure 2.1. The window allows you to select one of three types of setup – *Quick, Custom* or *None.*

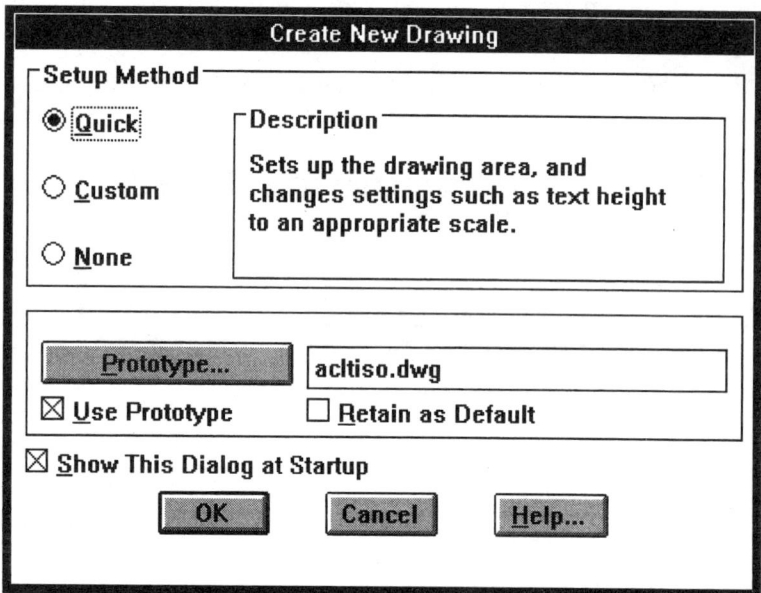

```
┌──────────────────────────────────────────────────────┐
│                  Create New Drawing                    │
│ ┌─Setup Method─────────────────────────────────────┐   │
│ │  ◉ Quick      ┌─Description────────────────────┐  │   │
│ │               │                                │  │   │
│ │               │ Sets up the drawing area, and  │  │   │
│ │  ○ Custom     │ changes settings such as text  │  │   │
│ │               │ height to an appropriate scale.│  │   │
│ │               │                                │  │   │
│ │  ○ None       └────────────────────────────────┘  │   │
│ └───────────────────────────────────────────────────┘   │
│ ┌───────────────────────────────────────────────────┐   │
│ │   ▓▓▓ Prototype... ▓▓▓    │ acltiso.dwg         │  │   │
│ │  ☒ Use Prototype        ☐ Retain as Default    │   │
│ └───────────────────────────────────────────────────┘   │
│ ☒ Show This Dialog at Startup                          │
│        ▓ OK ▓      ▓ Cancel ▓     ▓ Help... ▓          │
└──────────────────────────────────────────────────────┘
```

Figure 2.1   Create New Drawing dialogue box.

Quick

Allows you to use AutoCAD LT's automatic setup features such as setting units of measurement (metric or imperial measurement, etc.), size of the drawing sheet and grid and snap settings. In Figure 2.2 you see a setup of decimal units, an A3 sheet size (420×297) and grid and snap settings of 10 units. New users should use this method of starting a new drawing.

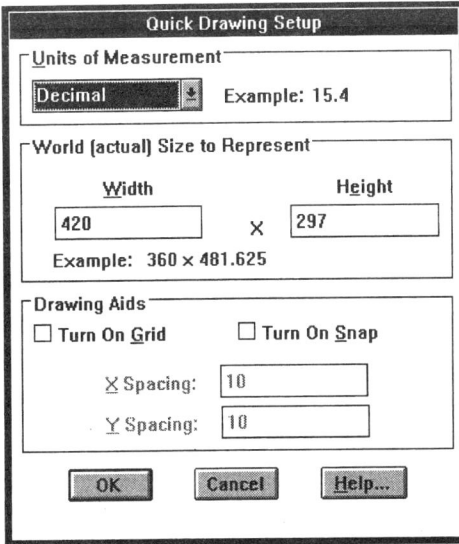

Figure 2.2   Quick Drawing Setup dialogue box.

Custom

Custom has the same facilities as *Quick* but with the added features of being able to insert a title block and border and use paper space features. Paper space and adding pre-drawn borders and title blocks are discussed more fully in Chapter 3. If you choose *Custom* setup a window appears as shown in Figure 2.3.This allows you to set up the units, drawing aids and title block.

None

As the name implies this gives you no options but goes directly into the drawing editor.

Setting Units Style

Remember that any button that includes a word with three trailing dots signifies that another dialogue box window will appear when that button is chosen. After using this dialogue box you will usually be transferred back up to the original dialogue box window. If you choose to alter the units the dialogue box appears as shown in Figure 2.4.

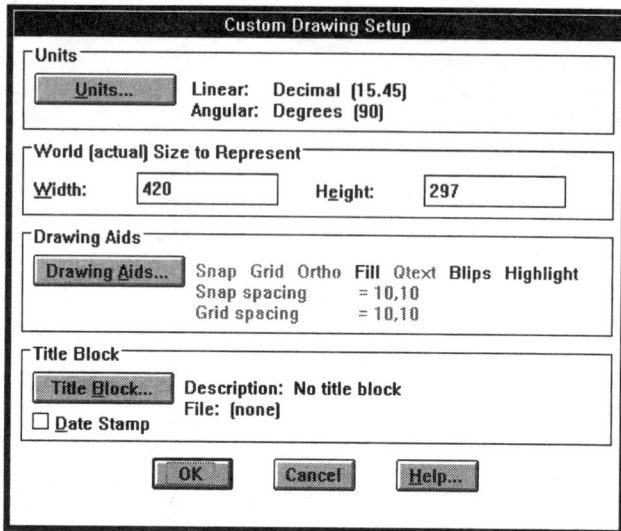

Figure 2.3   Custom Drawing Setup dialogue box.

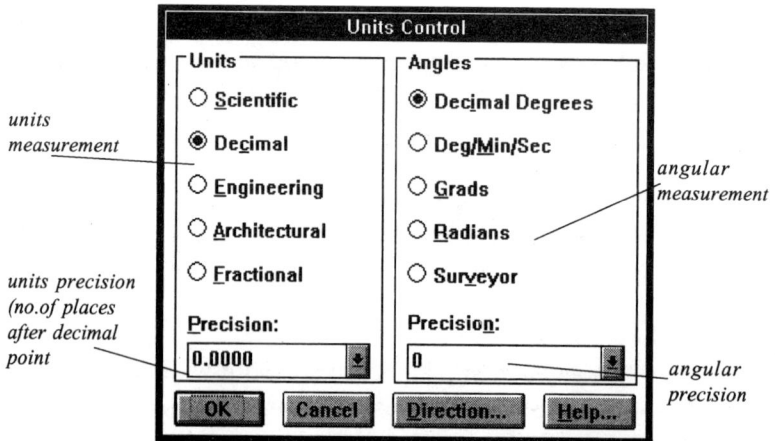

Figure 2.4   Units Control dialogue box.

Setting the Drawing Aids Style

The drawing aids dialogue box allows you to specify grid and snap values as shown in Figure 2.5. By entering the 'x' value and pressing Enter AutoCAD LT will amend the 'y' value to be the same as 'x'. If you require a rectangular grid you can change the 'y' value to suit and the grid will appear providing you have turned the grid on. Note that the grid does not appear on your hard copy.

The snap values can be changed using exactly the same method as for the grid. The snap values do not have to coincide with the grid. For example, if a grid size of 10 units is specified, the snap value could be set to 5, half of the grid value. You will then see the cursor snap or jump to the grid dots and also halfway between.

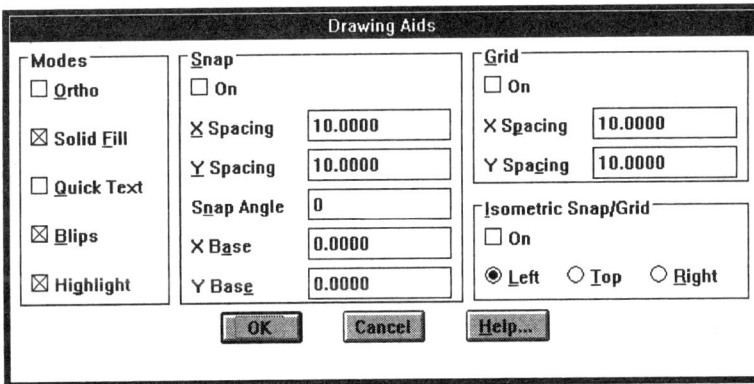

Figure 2.5   Drawing Aids dialogue box.

If you chose *Quick Setup* or *None* you can change the *Units Style* and *Drawing Aids* at any time in the drawing editor by using the *Settings* pull-down menu and *Units Style* or *Drawing Aids*.

Title Block

The Title Block button option in *Custom Setup* allows you to place a pre-drawn title block and border into the drawing. AutoCAD LT arrives with a number of title blocks and borders already prepared. You can also draw your own and place them into the drawing using this method. Figure 2.6 shows the AutoCAD LT pre-drawn borders.

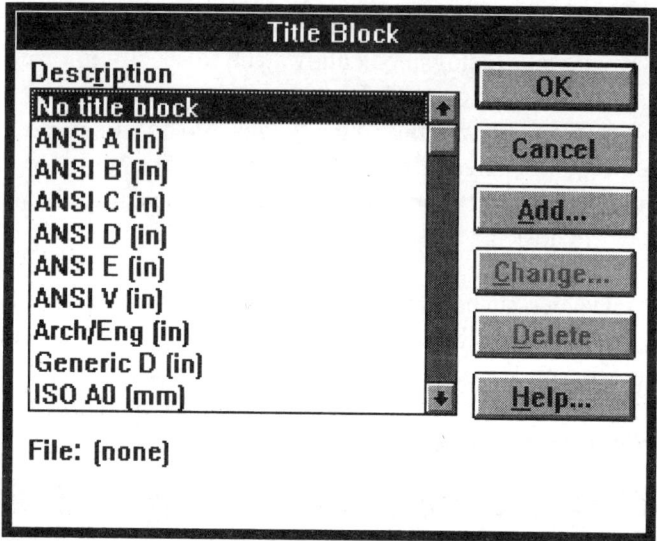

Figure 2.6   Title Block dialogue box with pre-drawn borders.

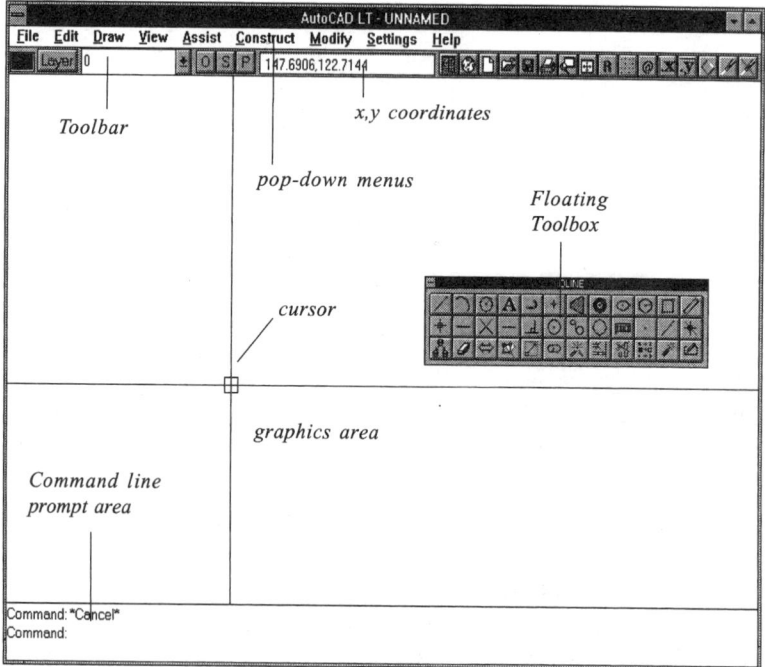

Figure 2.7   The AutoCAD LT graphics window.

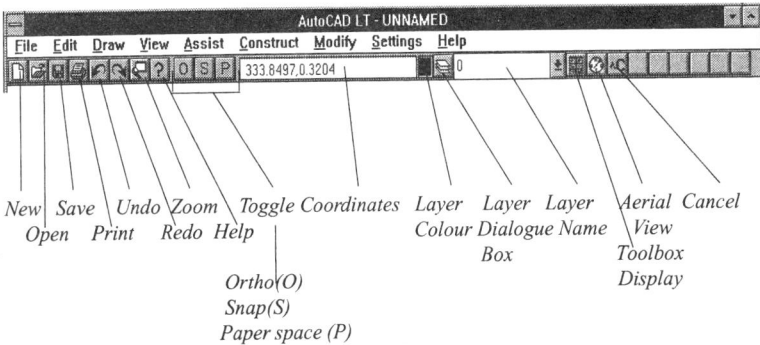

Figure 2.8   The Toolbar.

Once you have completed the initial setup the graphics window will appear as shown in Figure 2.7. Move your mouse and you will see that the cursor moves with a central target box at the intersection of the axes. The use of the features is covered in depth in Chapter 3. When you move the cursor into the Toolbar area it changes to a pointer and a rectangular bubble describing the function appears when the pointer is placed over a button or function. Figure 2.8 shows the Toolbar.

The Toolbar Explained

The maximum number of buttons allowed on the Toolbar is 26, in addition to the four preset buttons, but this depends on the resolution of your display. If the window size is reduced some buttons will not display.

New

Starts a new drawing and the *Create New Drawing* dialogue box appears as shown in Figure 2.1. This button has the same function as *File/New* and can be typed at the command line.

Open

Opens a previously saved drawing with the *Open Drawing* dialogue box. This button has the same function as the *File/Open* pull-down menu and can also be typed at the command line.

Save

This button saves the current drawing with a specified file name. It has the same function as the *File/Save* pull-down menu and can also be typed at the command line.

Print

The *Print* button brings up the *Print/Plot Configuration* dialogue box allowing an array of printing variations. Printing/Plotting is covered in depth in Chapter 5.

Undo

This button reverses the most recent operation. In fact, you can reverse right up until you last saved or opened the drawing. This function can also be accessed through the *Edit/Undo* pull-down menu.

Redo

If you use the *Undo* command and then need to reverse it, the *Redo* button will reinstate anything you did before you issued the *Undo* command. This function can also be accessed through the *Edit/Undo* pull-down menu.

Zoom

This button increases or decreases the screen view. This function can be accessed through the *View/Zoom* pull-down menu and is used extensively in the tutorial in Chapter 3.

Help

This button displays online help. This function can also be accessed through the *Help* pull-down menu.

Toggle Button

These three buttons comprise the *Ortho, Snap* and *Paper Space* buttons. *Ortho* allows only horizontal and vertical movement of the cursor. *Snap* constrains cursor movement to the specified increments set in the *Settings/Drawing Aids* dialogue box. The 'P' button switches from *Paper Space* to *Model Space*.

Coordinates   581.5076,256.4401

This part of the Toolbar displays the current cursor position in x,y coordinates. In our example the coordinates are displayed to four decimal places but this can be changed through the *Settings/Unit Style* dialogue box as shown in Figure 2.4.

Layer Colour

The current layer colour is displayed in this box. If you are using a white background on which to draw, any layer with white as the default colour will have objects reversed in colour, i.e. they will appear black in colour and this colour will appear in the Toolbar.

Layer Dialogue Box

This button displays the *Layer Control* dialogue box which can also be accessed through *Settings/Layer Control.*

Layer Name   0

Displays the name of the current layer. The down arrow expands the window and allows quick changing from one layer to another. When you change to a different layer with a different colour the *Layer Colour* button will change also.

Toolbox Display

The floating Toolbox, as the name suggests, can be moved around the screen to any position by clicking in its top horizontal bar and dragging. By clicking this button you can control the display and positioning of the Toolbox. It can be positioned on the left and right of the screen or at the last place it was visible. When displayed at the left and right of the screen it appears as shown in Figure 2.9.

Aerial View

This button opens up the *Aerial View* dialogue box which will display the entire drawing within the window. With the *Aerial View* you can rapidly locate and move to a position in the drawing. It is displayed in reverse as shown in Figure 2.10.

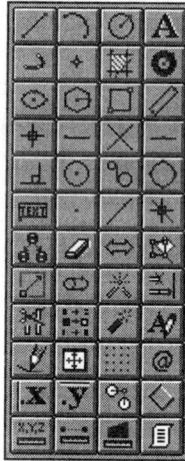

Figure 2.9   The Toolbox as it appears at the sides of the screen.

If you pick inside the *Aerial View* window and then use the right-hand mouse button, you can vary the size of the zoom window. At the same time the main drawing window changes to reflect the *Aerial View* as shown in Figure 2.11. Also available within this box is the ability to

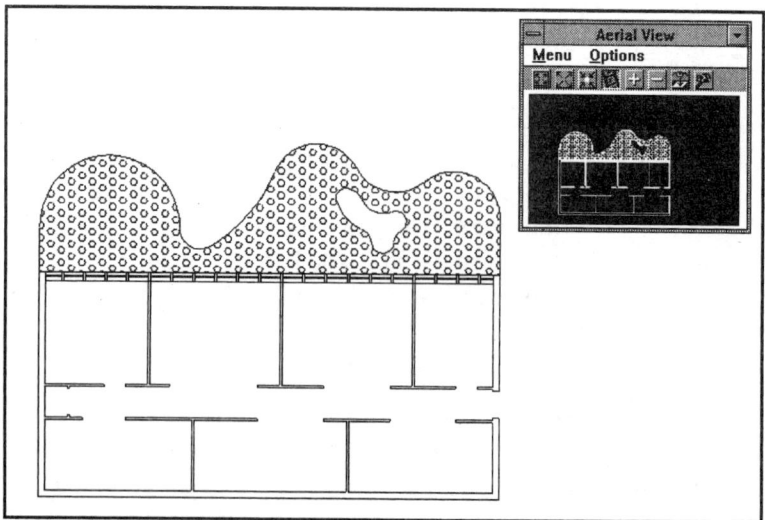

Figure 2.10   The Aerial View window.

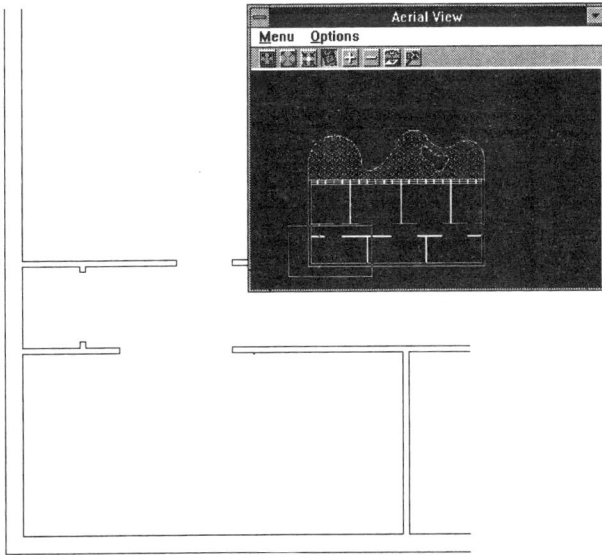

Figure 2.11   Using Zoom within the Aerial View window.

pan across the drawing along with the *Aerial View* buttons which include zooming extents, zooming by increments, matching the image to the graphics area and positioning the view within the Aerial View box window.

Cancel

If you have a low resolution monitor the ^C or *Cancel* command may not be displayed. Pressing this button will terminate in the middle of a process or complete a command. In dimensioning you will have to press the *Cancel* button twice to exit the command completely. This is extra to the normal exiting of dimensioning. Pressing *Ctrl+C* simultaneously also has the same effect.

Empty Buttons

These buttons are available for programming by placing the pointer over an empty button and clicking with the right mouse button. A dialogue box appears as shown in Figure 2.12. You can place text or an image in the button and in our example we have selected *Image* and *Boundary Hatch* in the selection window. At the AutoCAD LT

Command *'bhatch'* has been entered. *OK* this and the icon will appear on the Toolbar as shown in Figure 2.13.

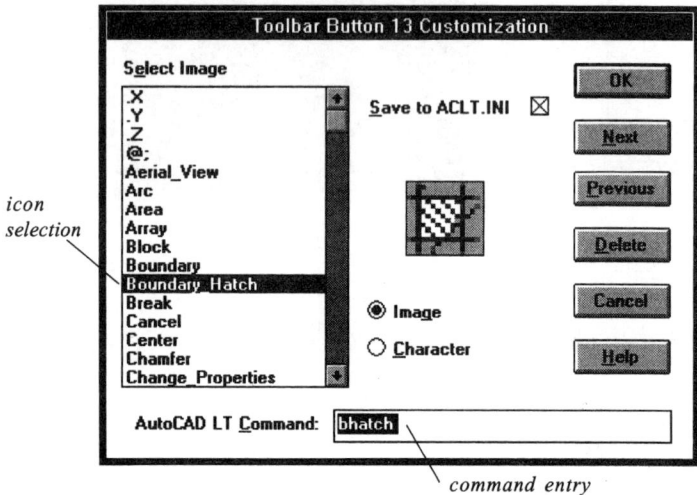

icon selection

Figure 2.12   Toolbar button customization dialogue box.

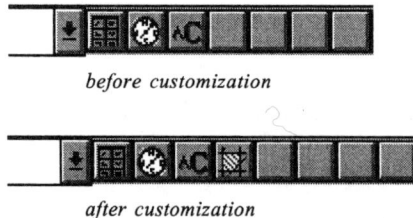

before customization

after customization

Figure 2.13   Progammable buttons showing before and after customization.

The Prototype Drawing

When you start a new drawing the dialogue box appears as shown in Figure 2.1. In this dialogue box is a button called *Prototype...* with the name of the template drawing which automatically loads when you start the new drawing. A template is a set of pre-defined values and the new drawing takes all of these values and incorporates them into the new drawing. Put simply, the untouched new drawing is a clone of the prototype. The drawing *acltiso.dwg* is the template or prototype which automatically loads its values into your new drawing. If you want to load a drawing other than *acltiso.dwg* click on *Prototype...* and a *Prototype Drawing File* dialogue box appears as shown in Figure 2.14. AutoCAD LT arrives with two protype drawings – *acltiso.dwg* and *aclt.dwg*. The *acltiso.dwg* is for ISO/Metric use while *aclt.dwg* is for American/English sheet sizes and units.

It follows therefore that we can create a template drawing and use it as a prototype. Your personalized prototype could include a border and related symbolization, blocks (blocks and creating blocks are discussed in Chapter 3), layers, linetypes and text styles.

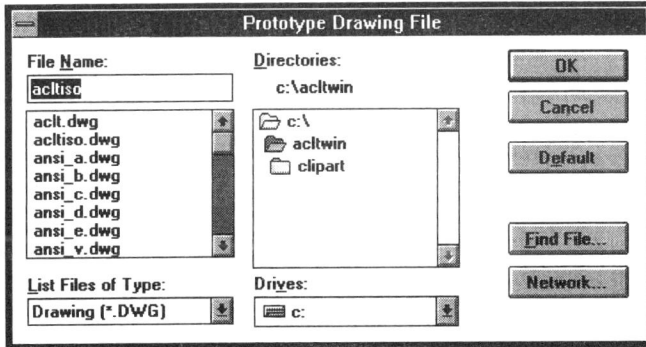

Figure 2.14   Prototype Drawing File dialogue box.

Creating a Personalized Prototype Drawing

1.   Start a new drawing.

2.   Add any new settings that will be needed for subsequent drawings. This could be loading linetypes, setting dimension and text styles, etc.

3.   Create any layers which will be needed for subsequent drawings. Remember that you can add to them in subsequent drawings.

4.   Draw a border and/or title block if needed.

5.   Do not draw any objects in the drawing that are not neces-
      sary.

6.   Save the drawing with a meaningful name that suggests it is a
      prototype drawing, e.g *proto1*.

7.   When you start a new drawing use the *Prototype...* button to
      load your personalized prototype drawing. Remember that you
      could retain your personalized prototype drawing by checking
      the *Retain as Default* box.

You can also specify a prototype drawing without actually specifically drawing one. This is generally known as the NEW=OLD method.
When you start a new drawing, in the drawing name box you specify
new drawing name=old drawing name. The new drawing will take
on all of the settings and properties of the old drawing including any
drawn objects, which you will need to erase to create a blank drawing sheet.

Dialogue Boxes

The Toolbar, Toolbox and pull-down menus are all visible commands
in the AutoCAD LT graphics window. For its more complex functions AutoCAD LT uses windows or dialogue boxes with which you
receive and give information. They are typical of a Windows-type
dialogue box where most of them have *OK*, *Cancel* and *Help* buttons
as shown in Figure 2.13.

Any command which is succeeded by three dots as in the pull-down
Settings/Units Style... means that a dialogue box will appear if you
choose that command.

Buttons

A button will initiate an immediate action. *OK* for example will close
a dialogue box and accept the values held there. *Cancel* will also
close a dialogue box but abandons any values.

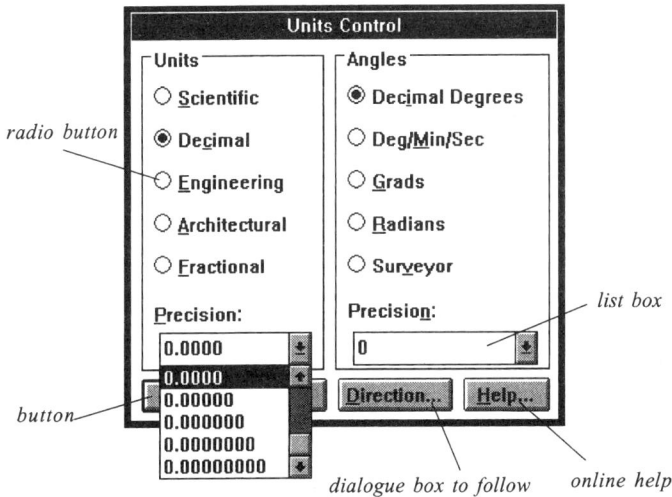

Figure 2.15   A typical dialogue box contents.

Radio Button
A radio button or option button is used to select from a number of options as shown in Figure 2.15. By selecting one, another button will be released from its function.

Check Box
Square check boxes are used to alter settings that have two values. A check or cross mark in the box means the value is either on or off.

Slider Bar
A slider bar is used to alter values within a range. You can either click on the slider bar button and drag it or click on the up and down arrow keys to adjust the value.

Text Box
Text boxes are areas bounded by a box in which text is typed. When you click on a text box a 'flashing' vertical bar awaits your input. You can highlight the text by double-clicking or by using the click and drag methods.

List Box

List boxes contain lists of items from which you choose. Figure 2.15 shows a list box containing the number of zeros of precision and can scroll up and down. The list box is opened and closed by the downwards pointing arrow at its side.

Online help

Online help can be accessed through the *Help* pull-down and contains very detailed descriptions of all the commands and dialogue box options. Procedures are included for the most common tasks such as drawing lines, etc.

After picking the question mark as shown in Figure 2.16, the *Help* dialogue box appears. Click on *Contents* and you are invited to type your query at the flashing cursor in the new dialogue box that replaces the one shown in Figure 2.16. An alternative to using the question mark is the *F1* key which brings up the same dialogue box. Using *Help* is covered in more detail in Chapter 3.

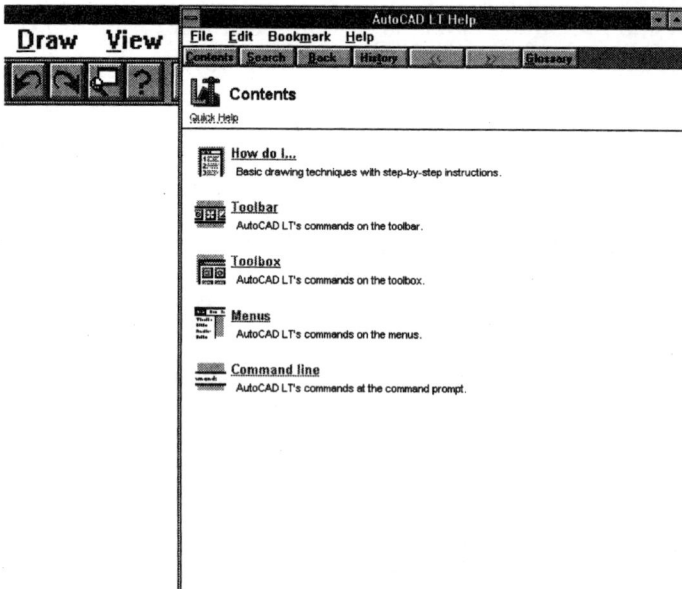

Figure 2.16   Help dialogue box and Toolbar access to Help.

The Command Line

The command line is where you enter commands and respond to requests by AutoCAD LT. The command line displays three lines of information, the current line and two previous lines called the command history. It is located in the bottom left-hand corner of the screen as shown in Figure 2.17. To view more lines of history you can switch to the text screen with the *F2* key.

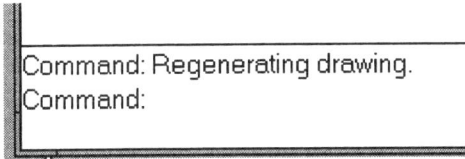

```
Command: Regenerating drawing.
Command:
```

Figure 2.17   The command line.

The Cursor Menu

The Cursor menu contains the object snap selections also found in the Toolbox as described in Chapter 3. It is accessed by the middle button on a three-button mouse or, if you have a two-button mouse, by pressing the *Shift* key and the *Return* button on the mouse simul-

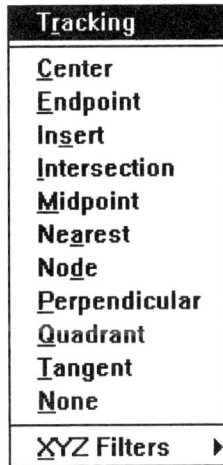

```
Tracking
Center
Endpoint
Insert
Intersection
Midpoint
Nearest
Node
Perpendicular
Quadrant
Tangent
None
XYZ Filters  ▶
```

Figure 2.18   The Cursor menu dialogue box.

taneously. The *Return* button is usually the right button. This brings up the dialogue box as shown in Figure 2.18. The use of these functions is described in the tutorial in Chapter 3.

The Concept of Layering Drawings

Layers are the equivalent of using overlays in manual drafting. They are used to group objects with similar properties or within the same function. Colours and linetypes can be added to aid on-screen clarity with colours also governing line width at plotting time.

Layers can be grouped for functionality as shown in Figure 2.19. Whenever you need to draw a broken line, for example (you would

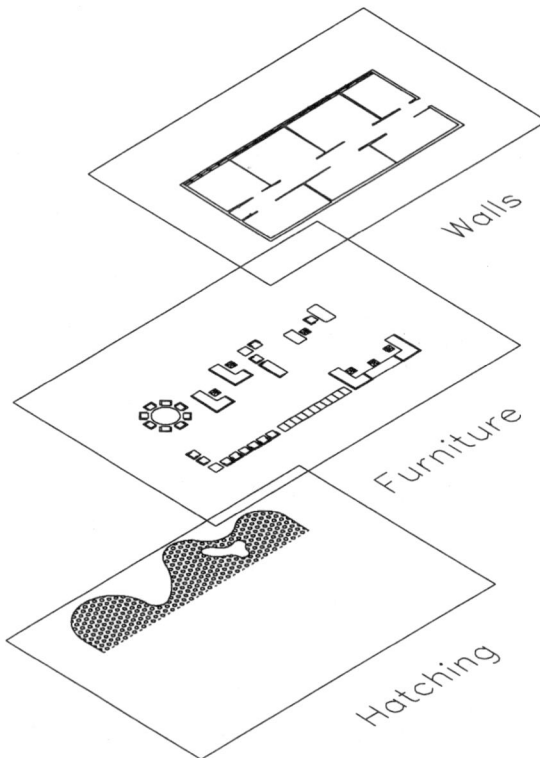

Figure 2.19   The concept of layering drawings.

previously have created a layer specifically for this feature and given it a meaningful name such as Hiddendetail, a colour, and assigned a linetype such as Hidden), that layer is made the current layer on which to draw and the line is drawn. It appears in the colour and linetype assigned to the layer Hiddendetail.

Creating a New Layer

You can use the button in the Toolbar with the layer icon as described in the Layer Dialogue Box section earlier in the chapter or use the *Settings/Layer Control* pull-down menu. The *Layer Control* dialogue box appears as shown in Figure 2.20. At the flashing cursor you can enter the new layer name and then click on *New*. The name will appear in the layer list with, at this stage, the colour of white and a Continuous linetype.

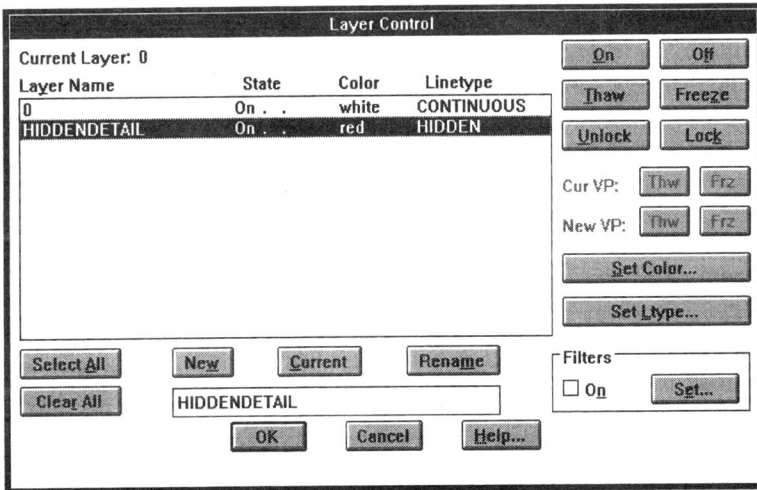

Figure 2.20   Layer Control dialogue box.

Changing the Layer Colour

To change the layer colour from the default white, click on the layer name that you wish to make active. It will become reversed as shown in Figure 2.20. The 'greyed out' buttons now become active. Click on the *Set Colour* button and the dialogue box is overlaid with the

Select Colour dialogue box as shown in Figure 2.21. Click on a colour and *OK* it. The dialogue box disappears and the new colour appears in the layer list.

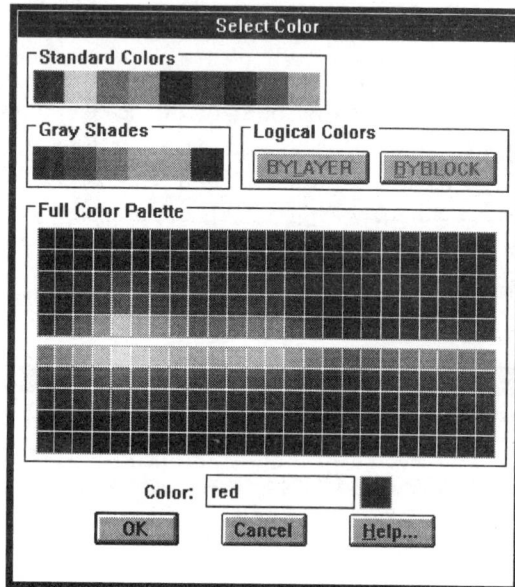

Figure 2.21   The Select Colour dialogue box.

Changing the Linetype Style

As with setting the colour, make the layer active, click on *Set Linetype* and the *Select Linetype* dialogue box will appear as shown in Figure 2.23. Pick the linetype that you require and *OK* it; the dialogue box disappears and the new linetype appears in the layer list.

You may have had only one linetype in the list – Continuous. That's because the prototype drawing, *Acltiso.dwg*, only loads the Continuous linetype. To load the linetypes you must exit the *Layer Control* dialogue box; using *Settings/Linetype Style/Load,* follow the instructions on the Command line. After typing the asterisk a dialogue box will appear as shown in Figure 2.22. Accept the default linetype file (*acltiso.lin*) and all of the linetypes in that file will be loaded.

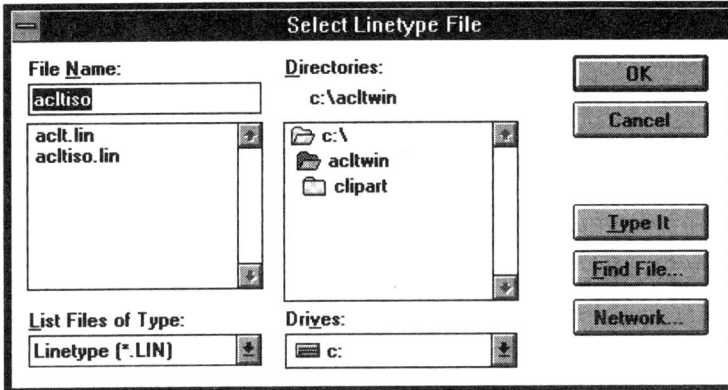

Figure 2.22 The Select Linetype File dialogue box.

Command:'_linetype
?/Create/Load/Set: L
linetypes to load: * (type in an asterisk – meaning 'all' the linetypes in the file)
Linetype BORDER loaded
Linetype BORDER2 loaded

Linetype PHANTOMX2 loaded
?/Create/Load/Set:Return

Re-activate the *Layer Control* dialogue box, select the layer to change, pick the *Set Linetype* button and you should see a full list of linetypes this time as shown in Figure 2.23.

Dimension Styles

The style of dimensions varies with the internal requirements of organizations and in AutoCAD LT you can save differing dimension styles with a name. The styles are accessed through the *Settings/Dimension Styles and Settings* dialogue box which is shown in Figure 2.24.

All dimensions are created using the current style; a style is created by naming the style, selecting settings for dimension lines, extension lines, arrowhead types and sizes, text location and format, and colours and then saving the settings. This style then becomes the current style. You can repeat this with different settings and saving with

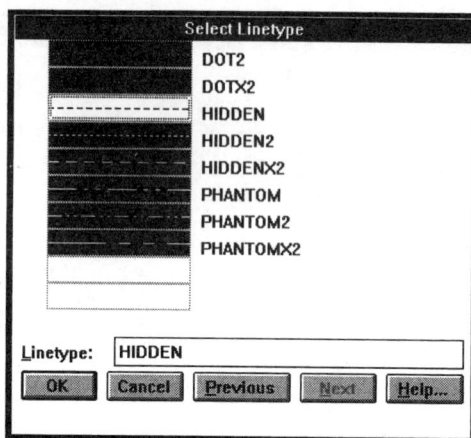

Figure 2.23 The Select Linetype dialogue box.

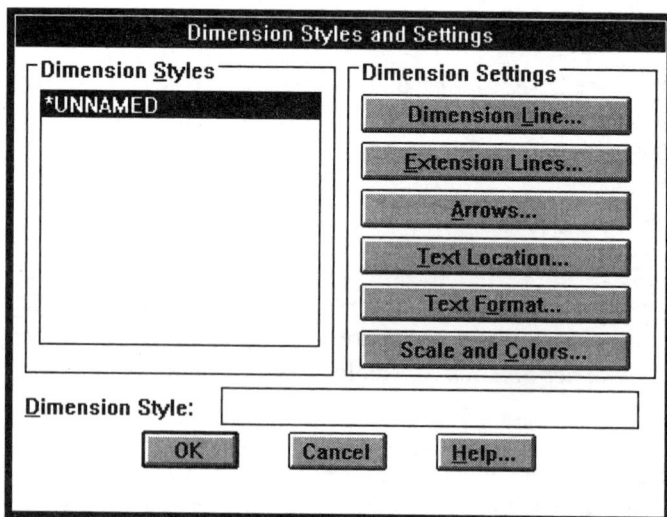

Figure 2.24 The Dimension Styles and Settings dialogue box.

a different name. Setting up dimension styles is covered in the tutorial in Chapter 3.

Saving and Exiting Drawings

The drawing can be saved at any time during drawing with the *File/Save* pull-down menu, the *Save* button, as described earlier in this chapter, or by typing 'save' at the command line. You can also save the current drawing under a different name by using *File/Save as* which produces the dialogue box as shown in Figure 2.25. Type the new name at the prompt and the original drawing still exists with an updated version under a different name.

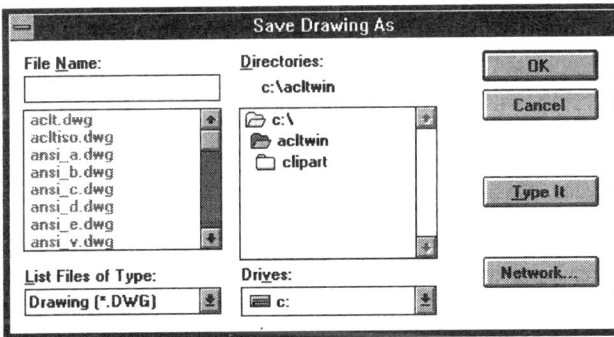

Figure 2.25   The Save Drawing As dialogue box.

Save allows you to continue in the drawing editor. *End* saves the drawing and quits the drawing editor. *Quit* leaves the drawing editor and does **not** save the drawing. Type *Save* at the command line or use the *File/Save* pull-down menu. The word *qsave* appears on the command line.

To exit the drawing use File/Exit from the pull-down menu or type *Exit* or *Quit* at the command line.

3 Starting to Draw

After you have double-clicked on the AutoCAD LT icon the AutoCAD LT logo and licensing information will appear as shown on page 2. This is followed by the drawing editor as shown in Figure 1.4 on page 3. You have an option here of either starting drawing immediately without giving the drawing a name and naming the drawing at a later time, or using *File/New* from the pull-down menu. Figure 3.1 shows the new drawing dialogue box. Remember that a maximum of eight characters are allowed for the drawing name which is a limitation imposed by the DOS operating system.

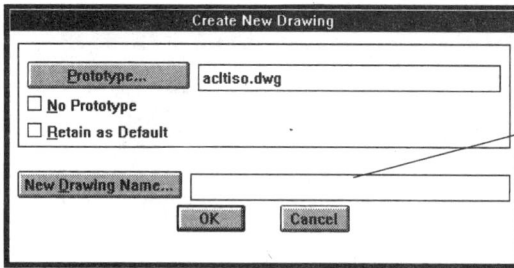

type the new drawing name here up to a maximum of 8 characters

Figure 3.1 Create New Drawing dialogue box.

If you start drawing immediately and save your drawing later with the *File/Save* pull-down menu or the Save Drawing button in the Toolbar a dialogue box appears as shown in Figure 3.2.

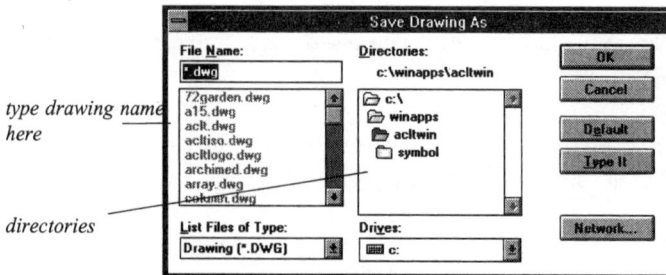

type drawing name here

directories

Figure 3.2 The Save Drawing As dialogue box.

Remember that the very first time you use this method to save your drawing the 'Save Drawing As' dialogue box appears. Subsequent savings come up with the 'qsave' message (quick save) on the command line.

The previously saved drawing names appear 'greyed out' which normally indicates that you cannot pick them. In AutoCAD LT, however, you can pick an existing drawing as shown in Figure 3.2 and it will subsequently appear on the File name edit box. This means of course that you will overwrite the previously saved file with whatever drawing you have on screen at that moment.

If you decide to close the drawing session by typing 'quit' at the command line or with the pull-down *Files/Exit* an alert dialogue box will appear as shown in Figure 3.3. If you do not save the changes you will lose all the updated information.

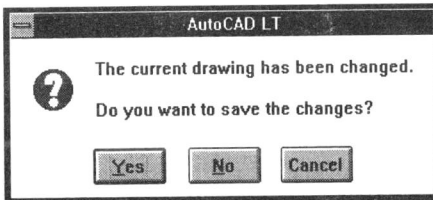

Figure 3.3   Alert dialogue box.

Using AutoCAD LT Help

When help is needed to explain or clarify, a full Help menu is included. In AutoCAD LT it is accessed through the Help pull-down as shown in Figure 3.4.

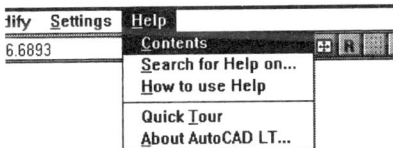

Figure 3.4   AutoCAD LT Help pull-down.

You can then search for a topic by clicking on *Search for Help on....* A dialogue box appears and in this example we are searching for the topic on drawing lines.

Type *Line* in the keyword text box and click on <u>*S*</u>*how Topics* as shown in Figure 3.5. The Topics list box will appear with a number of related topics concerning lines. Select *Line Command* and click on <u>*G*</u>*o To*. An explanation on drawing lines will appear. To close Help click on the Help Control menu bar and pick Close.

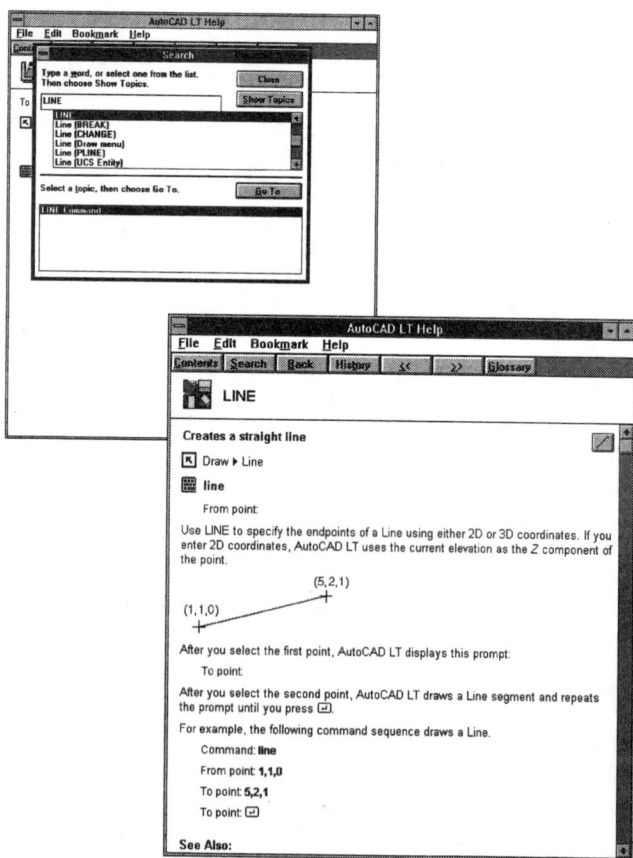

Figure 3.5   Help in detail.

The Help menu is extensive and can be used at any time during the editing session.

Tutorial

Getting Ready to Draw the Office Drawing

The following section is devoted entirely to creating a fictitious single storey block of small offices. You will be able to follow the instructions and commands and at the end of the session you will have created the target drawing as shown in Figure 3.6. You can save the drawing at any time and come back to where you left off.

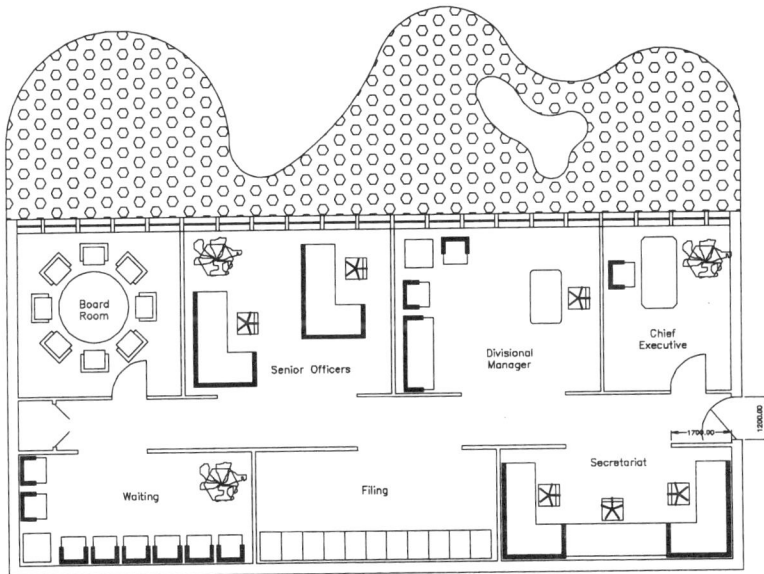

Figure 3.6   Tutorial target drawing.

You will learn how to use lines, polylines, arcs, hatching and dimensioning. Editing commands shown in Chapter 4 are covered in detail. Layering, discussed in Chapter 2, is put into practice. Creating blocks and inserting them is used extensively which will speed up your drawing significantly.

To Start the Session
Turn your computer on and activate AutoCAD LT as described in Chapter 1, pages 2 and 3.

When the drawing editor appears as shown on page 3 use the pull-down menu *Files/New*. Enter the name *Office* at the flashing cursor prompt opposite *New Drawing Name* and click on *OK* as shown in Figure 3.7. You have given your new drawing a name.

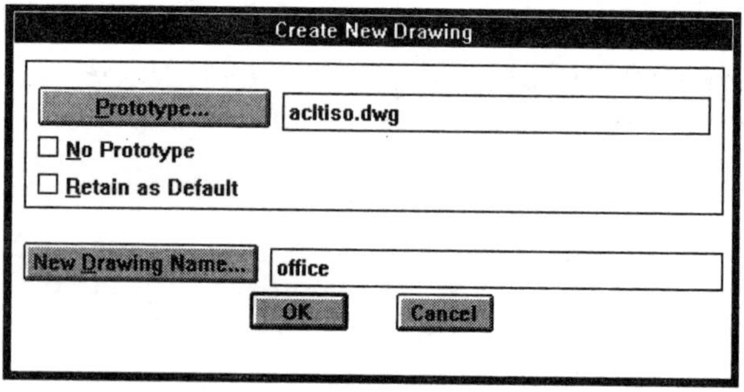

Figure 3.7   Naming the new drawing.

Units Command
You have to tell AutoCAD what units you are drawing in, metric or imperial, etc., so we will use the *Settings/Units Style* pull-down to set the preferences. Set units as decimal with two places of preci-

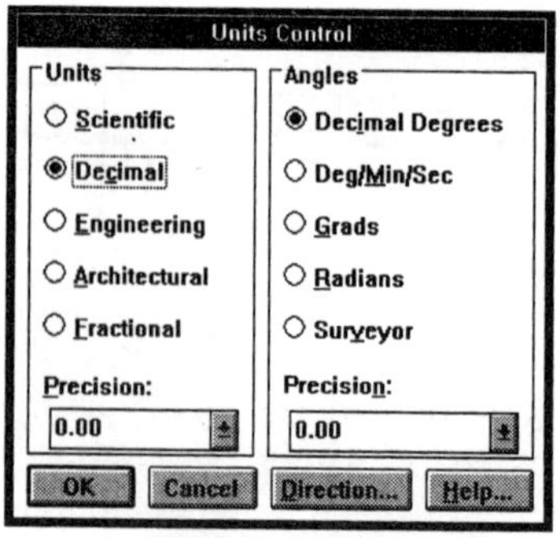

Figure 3.8   Setting the Units Style.

sion and angles as decimal, also with two places of precision as shown in Figure 3.8.

The units have to be set once only as AutoCAD LT will 'remember' the configuration for all subsequent drawings.

The Grid and Snap Commands

The *Grid* command places a grid of dots on the screen, with the distance between the dots set by you. The *Snap* command enables the cursor to 'jump' to a fixed increment. The snap increment can be greater, smaller or coincide with the grid increment.

To set the Grid and Snap values move to the pull-down menu and activate *Settings/Drawing Aids*; the dialogue box will appear as shown in Figure 3.9. Click in the value box adjacent to *X Spacing* and type in the value for the grid as 1000.00 and snap as 100. As each X value is placed, the Y value will automatically change as well. Click *OK* to leave the dialogue box and the values are set.

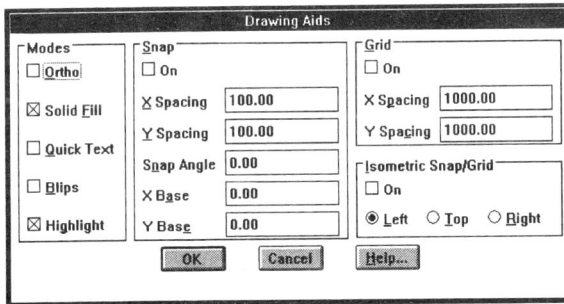

Figure 3.9 Setting the Grid and Snap values.

Grid and Snap are automatically activated when they are set with the dialogue box. Can you remember what function keys to use to turn them off? See page 8 for the answer. If you need a rectangular grid, enter a value in the 'Y coordinate box', and similarly for Snap. *Grid* and *Snap* can also be typed individually at the Command prompt, as can most AutoCAD LT commands.

The Limits Command

Generally speaking, drawings are always drawn to full size in AutoCAD LT, which is the opposite to manual drafting. Scaling takes place when the drawing is plotted and is discussed in Chapter 5.

To specify your drawing sheet size the *Settings/Drawings/Limits* command is used, with the bottom left-hand corner usually set at 0 units in the X, and 0 units in the Y as shown below.

```
Command: _Limits
Reset Model space limits:
ON/OFF<Lower left corner> <0.00,0.00>: Return
Upper Right Corner<420.00,297.00>: 30000,20000
```

To see all of the drawing sheet (you will not actually see the outline of a sheet) the *View/Zoom/All* command will have to be used and should be used every time the limits are changed:

```
Command: _Zoom
All/Center/Dynamic/Extents/Left/Previous/Window/<Scale(X)>: A
```

The Layer Command

Using layers in a drawing is similar to doing overlays in manual drafting as discussed in Chapter 2 . By placing items on different layers, many different kinds of drawings can be produced by making layers visible or invisible.

The easiest method of creating and managing layers is through the *Settings/Layer Control* pull-down menu or with the *Layer* button in the Toolbar; the dialogue box that appears is shown in Figure 3.10. The layers to create are listed below:

Layer name	Colour
Cabinet	Yellow
Chair	Red
Dimensions	Red
Doors	Green
Exechair	Red
Hatch	Green
Patioedge	Blue
Table	Yellow
Text	Cyan
Walls	Magenta
Windows	Cyan
Workstat	Yellow

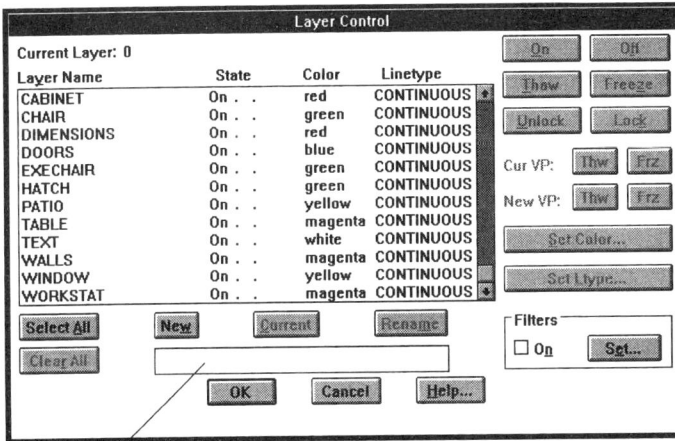

Enter new layer name here

Figure 3.10 The Layer Control dialogue box.

The dialogue box shows all the layers created, but your dialogue box shows only one layer, Layer 0.

Create all the layers shown by entering each new name, one at a time, at the flashing cursor, and then clicking on *New;* each name will be added to the list. Use the slider bar to see all the layers you have entered.

To change a layer colour (it automatically defaults to white) highlight the layer name by clicking anywhere along its line (the whole line will change colour to show that it is selected) and then click on *Set Color*. A *Select Color* dialogue box will appear as shown in Figure 3.11. Click on any of the *Standard Colors* and then *OK* it. The new colour will appear in the layer selected. Repeat this for all the layers.

Set the *Current Layer* to *Walls* by highlighting the *Walls* layer and click in the *Current* box.

Click on *OK* at the bottom of the Layer Control dialogue box when finished. If the Status line does not have the layer *Walls* shown, you have not made *Walls* the current layer.

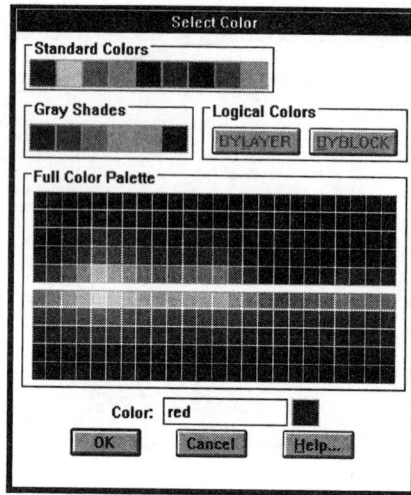

Figure 3.11 Select Colour dialogue box.

The Save, End and Quit Commands

Now is a good opportunity to save the drawing.

Save allows you to continue in the drawing editor. *End* saves the drawing and quits the drawing editor. *Quit* leaves the drawing editor and does **not** save the drawing. Type *Save* at the command line or use the *File/Save* pull-down menu. The word *qsave* appears on the command line.

It is good practice to save your drawing at regular intervals. Get into the habit of saving, say, every half-hour, or more often if necessary.

We are now ready to start drawing.

Drawing with Absolute Coordinates

Assuming that 0,0 is the bottom left-hand corner of the drawing sheet, use *Draw/Line* from absolute coordinates 1000,4000 (1000 in the positive X direction and 4000 in the positive Y direction) and complete the outline of the building as shown in Figure 3.12.

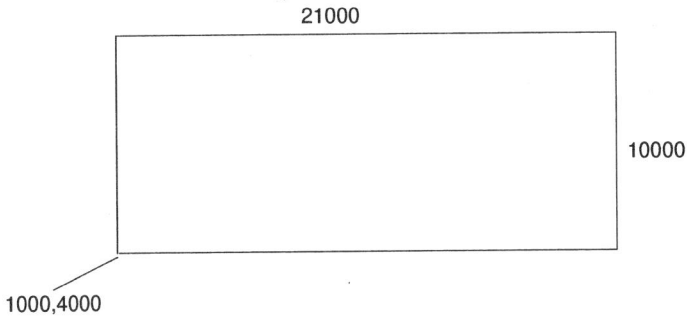

21000

10000

1000,4000

Figure 3.12 Absolute coordinates.

Drawing with Relative Coordinates

Relative coordinates are distances or directions from the last point that AutoCAD has stored in its memory. The last point can be accessed by the @ symbol.

To draw the right internal wall using relative coordinates start with *DRAW/Line* again and the response will be:

> *From point:* **1300,4300**
> *To point:* **@20400,0**
> *To point:* **@0,9700**
> *To point:* **Return**

To draw the left internal wall:

> *From point:* **1300,4300**
> *To point:* **@0,9700**
> *To point:* **Return**

Drawing with Polar Coordinates
But first – How AutoCAD LT handles angles

Polar coordinates require the input of a distance (from the last point) and an angle in the x-y plane. The symbol for the angle is the 'less than' sign < and is written *@distance<angle value*. The default direction for angles is anticlockwise as shown in Figure 3.13.

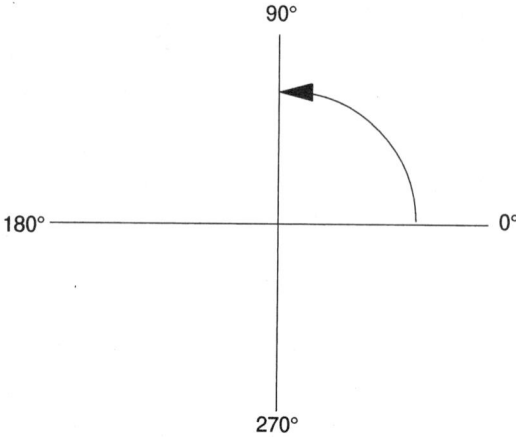

Figure 3.13 Angular measurement. Angles measured anti-clockwise.

To draw one edge of the central partition wall as shown in Figure 3.14 with polar coordinates select *Draw/Line:*

> *From point:* **1000,9000**
> *To point:* **@21000<0**
> *To point:* **Return**

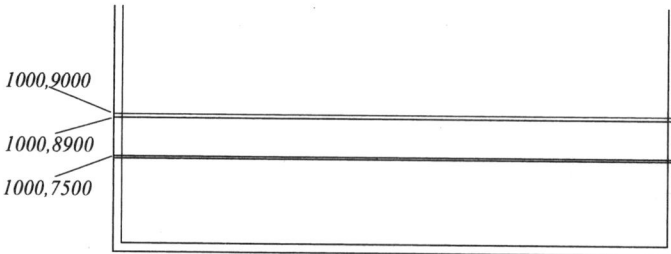

Figure 3.14 The central partition wall drawn with polar coordinates.

To draw the other edge:

> *From point:* **1000,8900**
> *To point:* **@21000<0**
> *To point:* **Return**

To draw the other side of the corridor (Figure 3.14):

> *From point:* **1000,7500**
> *To point:* **@21000<0**
> *To point:* **Return**

and the other edge:

> *From point:* **1000,7400**
> *To point:* **@21000<0**
> *To point:* **Return**

Draw the window wall with:

> *From point:* **1000,13600**
> *To point:* **@21000<0**
> *To point:* **Return**

as shown in Figure 3.15.

Draw one partition wall:

> *From point:* **6000,14000**
> *To point:* **@5000<270**
> *To point:* **Return**
> *From point:* **6100,14000**
> *To point:* **@5000<270**
> *To point:* **Return**

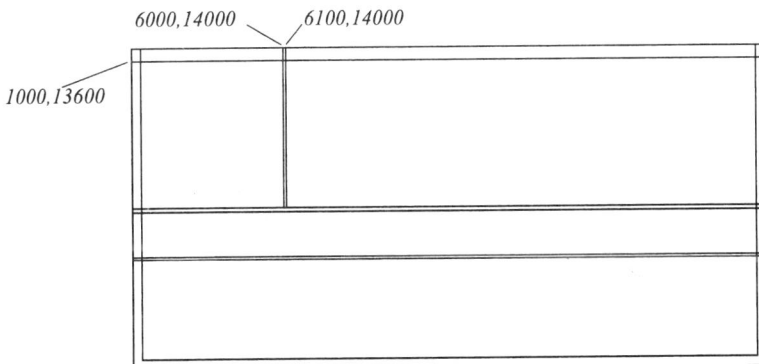

Figure 3.15 Drawing the window wall and partition with polar coordinates.

The room widths are 5900 mm. Draw in the two remaining partitions as shown in Figure 3.16 using either relative or polar coordinates. Remember to start the line with an absolute coordinate.

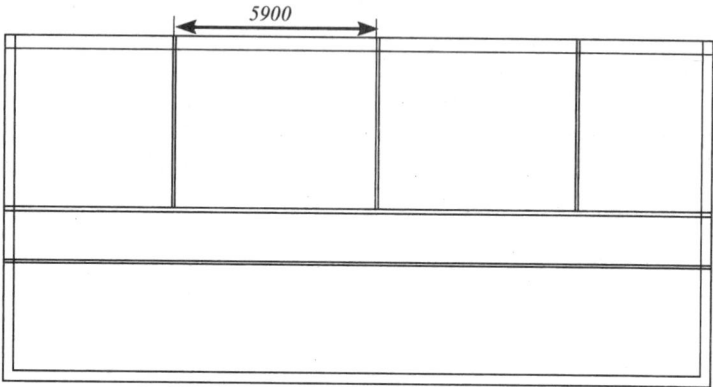

Figure 3.16   Drawing the partitions.

Draw one edge of the partition wall to the south side of the corridor.

From point: **8000,7400**
To point; **@3100<270**
To point: **Return**

The partition is 100 mm wide. Draw in its partner using polar coordinates. The room widths are 6900 mm. Draw the remaining partition using relative coordinates as shown in Figure 3.17.

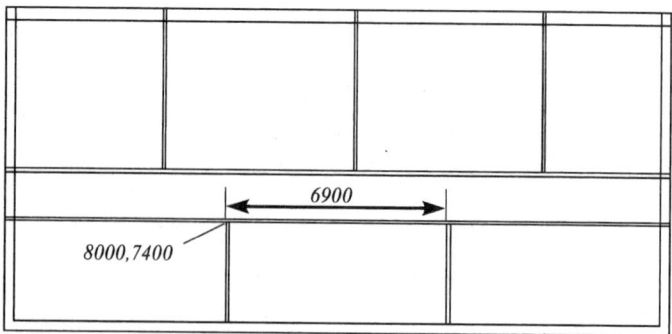

Figure 3.17   Finishing the partition walls.

Next, we are going to add the door reveals. Activate the *Grid* and *Snap* with the F7 and F9 function keys respectively. Remember that we have previously set the grid increment to 1000 mm and the snap increment to 100 mm.

The Zoom Command

The Zoom command manipulates the screen display of your drawing image. You can zoom in to show more detail, or zoom out for a 'bird's eye' view. Zoom only changes the screen view — it does not alter the scale or size of the drawing.

We are going to zoom in on a portion of the drawing so that the door reveals can be added accurately. After *Zoom/View/Window* is completed your new screen view will display only the shaded area shown in Figure 3.18.

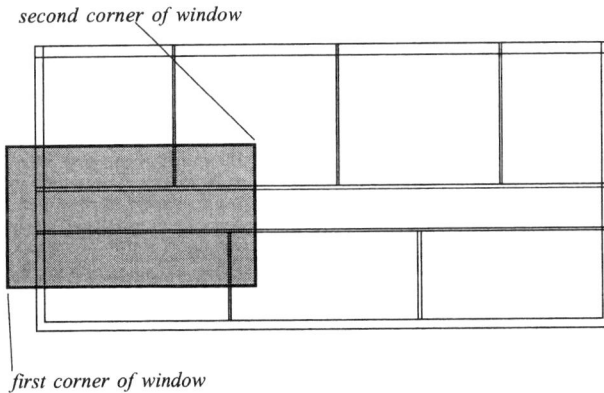

second corner of window

first corner of window

Figure 3.18 Using the Zoom command.

Use *View/Zoom/Window* from the pull-down:

> *All/Center/Dynamic/Extents/Left/Previous/Vmax/Window/<Scale(X/XP)>:*
> *First corner: **pick** first corner Other corner: **pick** second corner*

If you use the keyboard to activate any of the **Zoom** options rather than the pull-down, only the first letter — z — has to be typed, followed by the first letter of the option. This is known as an alias. Your view should now look like the area shown in Figure 3.18.

The Modify and Construct Commands

Editing covers a wide range of commands and, next to drawing, will probably be the most used command.

Note that when any of the editing functions are selected, the cursor changes to a square called a pickbox as shown in Figure 4.1. It is advisable at this point to refer to Chapter 4 as you are working through the editing because it gives full explanations of the editing functions.

The Trim Command

We will first trim the unwanted overlapping wall lines that we constructed earlier. Use *Modify/Trim* and choose the cutting edge to start as shown in Figure 3.19.

> *Select cutting edge(s)*
> *Select Objects:* **pick** *the object as shown in Figure 3.19 (1 found)*
> *Select Objects:* **Return**
> *Select objects to trim:* **pick** *as shown*

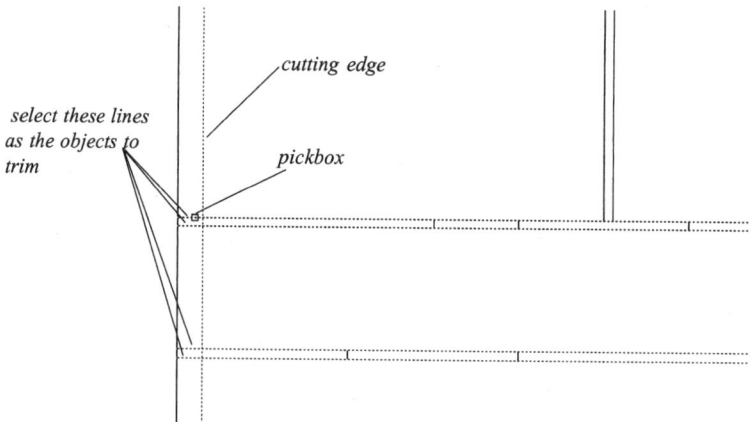

Figure 3.19   Trimming the wall lines.

The Pan Command

The *Pan* command allows you to move the screen image from one part of the drawing to another. To pan the drawing, you first indicate the displacement by picking the 'from point' and then the 'to point'. You can give these points as coordinates but generally the pointing method is used. Use *View/Pan* to move to the other side of the drawing.

Displacement: **pick** *Second point:* **pick**

Pan around the drawing and with reference to Figure 3.20 draw in the door reveals. Remember that as the grid and snap are activated you should be able to locate the positions easily. When you have completed this, *View/Zoom/All* to show all of the drawing and then *View/Zoom/Window* similar to as shown in Figure 3.21.

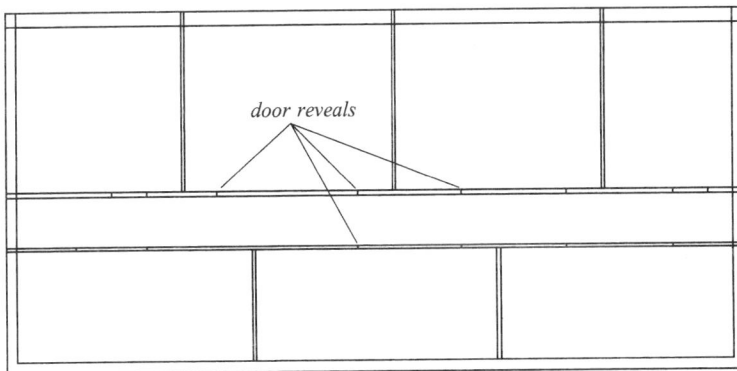

door reveals

Figure 3.20 Positioning the door reveals.

The Break Command

The Break command can be used to erase part of a line, polyline, a circle, polygon or an arc. You can also use it to cut an object without erasing any part of it as shown in Chapter 4.

Use *Modify/Break*

Select objects: **pick** *wall line as shown*
Enter second point(or F for first): **F**
Enter second point: **pick** *other side of door reveal.*

Pan your way around the drawing and *Break* the doorways and wall junctions. The results of *Break* are shown in Figure 3.22.

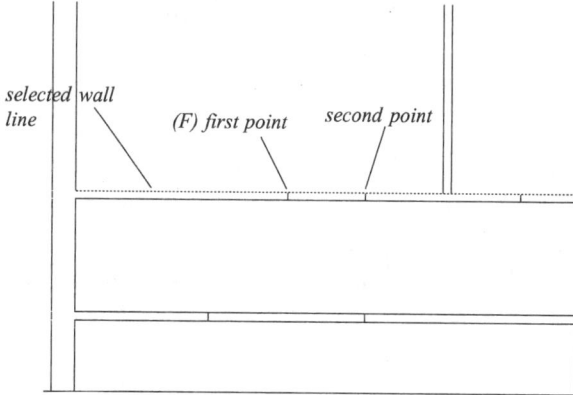

Figure 3.21   Before breaking the reveal.

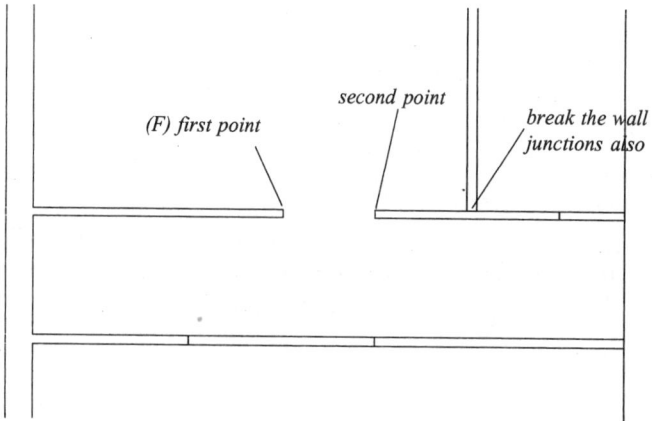

Figure 3.22   After breaking the reveal.

The Array Command

The Array command repeats an object in a rectangular or circular pattern. Rectangular arrays are made up of columns and rows and the spaces between each unit. We will use the rectangular array to draw the window mullions.

Use *Settings/Layer Control* to set the current layer to Windows. *View/Zoom/Window* to the area shown in Figure 3.23.

We will draw in two mullions as shown in Figure 3.23. Use *Draw/ Line:*

> *From point:* **2000,14000**
> *To point:* **@400<270**
> *To point:* **Return**
> *From point:* **200,1400**
> *To point:* **@400<270**
> *To point:* **Return**.

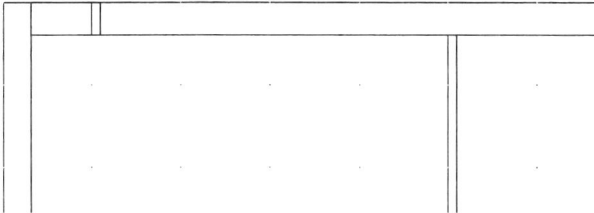

Figure 3.23 The enlarged top left corner of the drawing.

Use *Modify/Array:*

> *Select Objects:* **select** *the two vertical lines you have just drawn*
> *Rectanglar or Polar(R/P):* **R**
> *Number of rows(---)<1>:* **1**
> *Number of columns(|||)<1>:* **20**
> *Distance between columns:* **1000**

View/Zoom/All and you will see the mullions in their correct positions as shown in Figure 3.24.

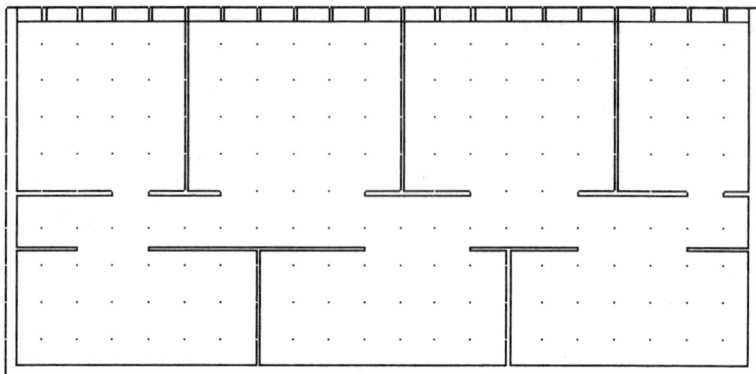

Figure 3.24   The completed rectangular array.

Object Snap – A New Tool

So far we have drawn with the aid of coordinates. But what happens when we don't know a coordinate value? AutoCAD LT provides us with a tool called *object snap* which allows us to pick specific points on objects such as endpoints, midpoints and centres of circles and arcs, for example.

Access to object snap is through the *Assist/Object Snap* pull-down menu as shown in Figure 3.25 where the dialogue box allows us to set a snap mode permanently. You can also type *osnap* at the key-

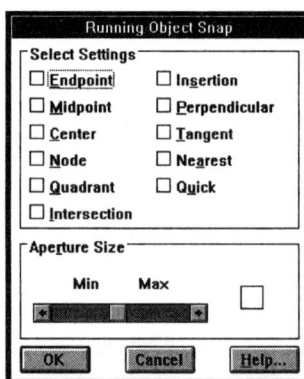

Figure 3.25   Running Object snap modes.

board. After an Osnap mode is chosen, the cursor changes to a cursor with a target at its centre. This command is known as the *Osnap override*, because it will override a standard object snap. A standard or permanent object snap can be set by typing *Osnap<mode>* followed by choosing endpoint, for example. Every time an entity is drawn after this is done, it will have the target box attached to the cursor, 'looking' for an endpoint of a previously drawn object to which to attach the new object. To cancel a permanent object snap, type *Osnap<mode>none* at the command line and it clears the setting.

There are a few rules in placing the target box in the various object snap overrides and each will be described as it occurs.

The most convenient method of setting a single object snap is through the Toolbox as shown in Figure 3.26. After activating the line command move the cursor to the Toolbox where it will change to a pointer, pick the desired object snap and you will see that snap value appear on the command line as shown below where we are drawing the centreline of the window glass.

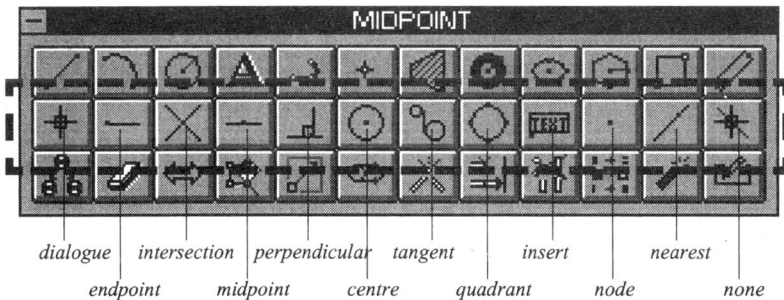

dialogue | intersection | perpendicular | tangent | insert | nearest
endpoint | midpoint | centre | quadrant | node | none

Figure 3.26 Object snap modes in the Toolbox used for a single object snap.

Object snap – MIDpoint
Use *View/Zoom/Window* to get to the area shown in Figure 3.27 in readiness for producing the glass between the mullions. Once the glass is drawn, it will be arrayed in the same way as the mullions.

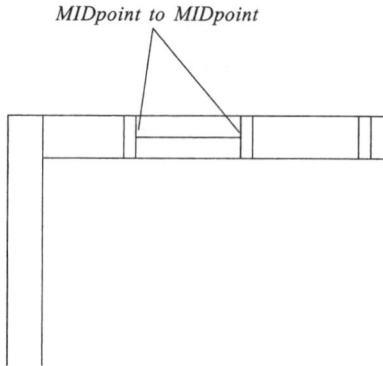

Figure 3.27 Using Object Snap — midpoint.

Use *Draw/Line:*

> *From point:* **MIDpoint** *of the mullion as shown*
> *To point:* **MIDpoint** *of the other mullion*
> *To point:* **Return**

The Offset Command

The *Offset* command copies lines and arcs parallel to the chosen entity. In this example we will form the inner and outer edges of the window glass with *Offset*, remove the central line and finally array the glass along the wall. Use *Modify/Offset*:

> *Offset distance or Through<Through> 25*
> *Select object to offset: pick the line*
> *Side to Offset?: pick anywhere above the line*
> *Select object to offset: pick the line again*
> *Side to offset?: pick anywhere below the line*

The *Through* option of *Offset* asks you to select an object and a point through which that object must pass. The *Offset* command repeats so you can continue selecting objects at the offset distance or through new points.

Modify/Erase the (central) construction line (Figure 3.28). Remember to disable snap (F9):

Select objects: **pick** *the central line*
Select objects: **Return**

Modify/Array/Rectanglar both edges of the window glass with 1 row, 19 columns, and a distance of 1000 mm between each column.

View/Zoom/All as shown in Figure 3.29 and you will see that the two end windows are not yet glazed.

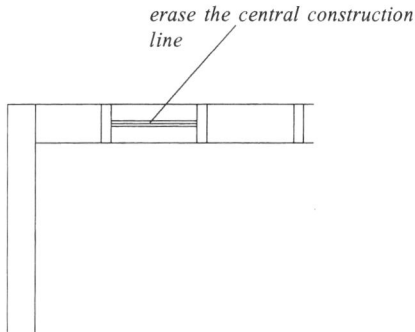

Figure 3.28 Erasing the central construction line.

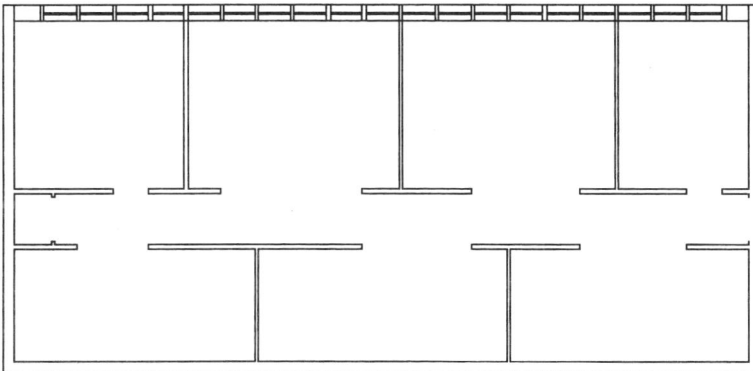

Figure 3.29 Arraying the window glass.

Object Snap – PERPendicular

To construct the remaining glazing we will use the same method as
before. The difference this time is that we must use *PERPendicular*
for the second line as shown in Figure 3.30. If we used *MIDpoint*
for both lines, the resulting line would be in the midpoint of the long
wall. Why is this? Try it with *MIDpoint* for both to see the result,
erase it and repeat with *PERPendicular.*

Use *Draw/Line:*

> *From point:* **MIDpoint** *of the first line*
> *To point:* **PERPendicular** *to the second line.*
> *To point:* **Return**

Modify/Offset this line as before to both sides and erase the mid
line. Complete glazing the windows by repeating this operation on
the remaining window at the right edge of the wall. *View/Zoom/All*
to check glazing is correct.

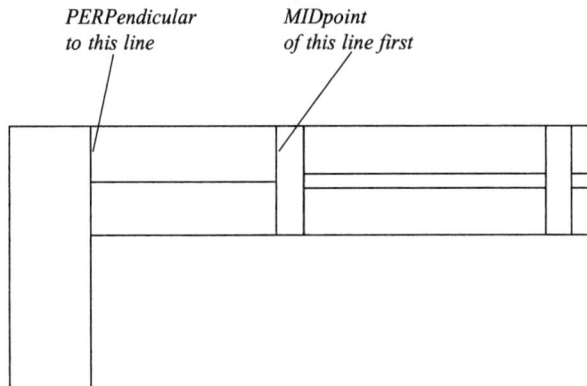

Figure 3.30 Object snap – perpendicular and midpoint.

The Copy Command
Object Snap – ENDpoint

We will now construct the cupboard at the left-hand side of the corridor. The *Copy* command is similar to *Move* but it leaves the original entity and allows more than one copy within the command as
described more fully in Chapter 4.

Use *Modify/Copy:*

> *Select Objects:* **pick** *the line as shown*
> *<Base point or Displacement>/Multiple:* **pick** *the* **ENDpoint** *of the line as shown.*
> *Second point of Displacement:* **@1000,0**

Modify/Offset the copied line by 100 mm in the direction shown in Figure 3.31 to form the partition.

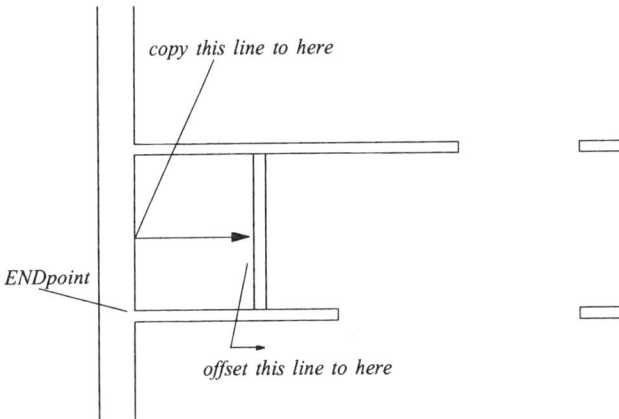

Figure 3.31 Copying and Offsetting.

When using *ENDpoint* the target does not have to enclose the end-point of the object – it can be placed anywhere between halfway and the desired endpoint.

The ID Command
Object Snap – INTersection
ID gives the coordinates of a point you select or places a blip at a coordinate location you specify. We will use *ID* to pick the *INTersection* of the new wall with the existing one and then draw a line relative to that point. But first, use the *Break* command to erase the junctions of the new wall with the existing wall.

Use *Inquiry/ID:*

> *Point:* **INTersection** *of the walls as shown*

The result will be a message giving the X,Y,Z coordinates of that point:

        X:2300.00   *Y:7500.00*   *Z:0.00*

Draw/Line:

        From point: **@0,100**
        To point: **PERPendicular** to the other side of the partition.

Modify/Offset this line by 1200 mm to form the other door reveal as shown in Figure 3.32.

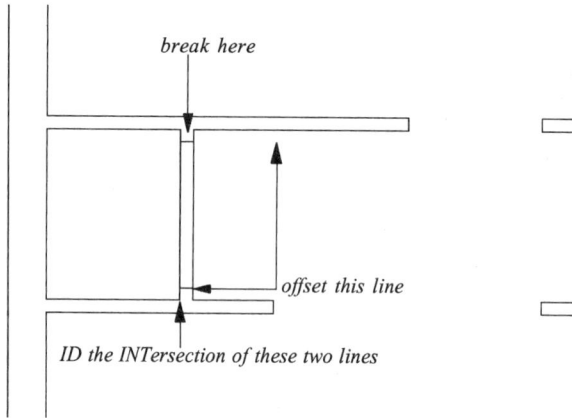

Figure 3.32 The ID and Object snap – intersection commands.

When using *Object snap/INTersection* the selected intersection must be within the target box.

The Mirror Command

The *Modify/Mirror* command allows us to make a mirror image of an object. The location of the new image is controlled by the axis about which the object is mirrored as described more fully in Chapter 4.

But first, *Modify/Break* the walls between the door jambs as shown. Activate *Settings/Layer Control* and make Doors the current layer. Turn *Ortho* on (F8). *Draw/Line* from the *MIDpoint* of the rear cupboard wall, as shown in Figure 3.33. Its length is not critical.

Draw/Line from the *MIDpoint* of the door jamb as shown in Figure 3.33, 600 mm long at 45°.

Use *Modify/Mirror:*

> *Select objects:* **pick** *door as shown*
> *First point of mirror line:* **pick** *one end of the horizontal construction line*
> *Second point:* **pick** *the other end of the line*
> *Delete old objects<N>:* **N**

Modify/Erase the construction line.

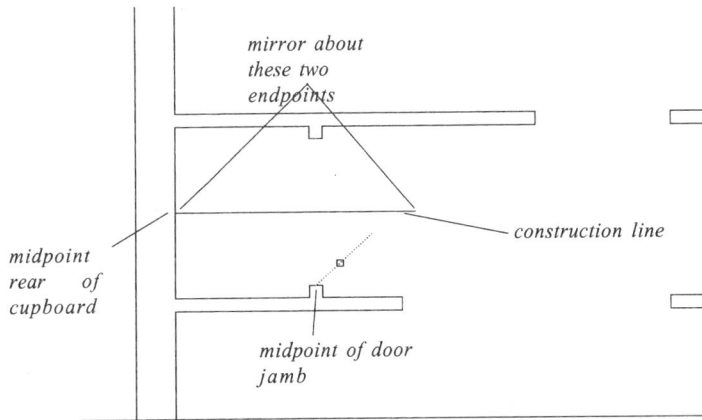

Figure 3.33   The Mirror command.

The Arc Command

The Arc command draws a segment of a circle. You can specify three items: a starting point, an ending or a centre point, and one other option which can be an angle, a radius chord, a direction or a second point. We will use an arc to draw the doorways in the office as shown in Figure 3.34. Use *Settings/Layer Control* and make Doors the current layer. Use *Draw/Line* to draw a vertical line 900 mm long from the *INTersection* of the jamb and wall to represent the door. Use *Draw/Arc* from the pull-down and select *SER* (Start, End, Radius).

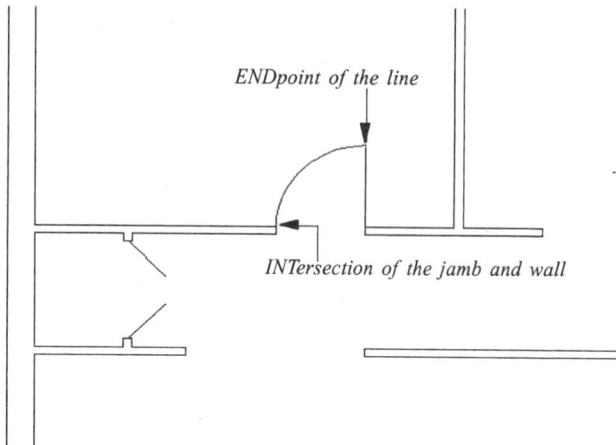

Figure 3.34   The arc command.

Arc/Center/<Start point>: pick endpoint of the door.
Center/End/<Second point>: E
End point: pick the INtersection of the jamb and wall as shown.
Angle/Direction/Radius/<Center point>:
R Radius: 1000

Repeat this operation for the other door.

Object Snap – NEARest

Next, we will draw the external door at the end of the corridor as shown in Figure 3.35. Turn *Snap* (F9) on and draw in the horizontal door jambs 100 mm from both internal walls as shown. We will now use *Draw/Arc/CSA* (Centre, Start, Angle) to draw the arc of the door. Use *Draw/Arc/CSA:*

ARC/Center/<Start point>: C Center: MIDpoint of jamb as shown
Start point: MIDpoint of jamb as shown
Angle/Length of chord/<End point>: A
Included angle: 90

and the arc is drawn. *Draw/Line* from the *MIDpoint* of the door jamb:

From point: Midpoint of – pick the bottom door jamb
To point: NEARest to – pick a point on the arc as shown
To point: Return

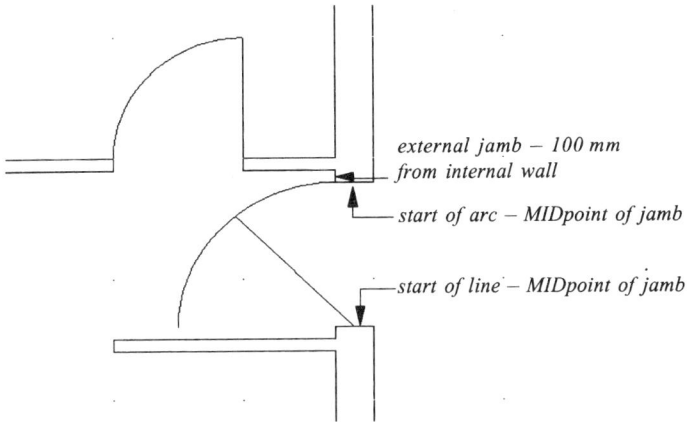

Figure 3.35 The Object snap nearest command.

Nearest is the point *visually* closest to the crossing point at the cursor centre so you will realize that it is not very accurate.

The Save Command
This is a reminder that you should have been saving the drawing regularly since you started drawing!

The Plan so Far
Your plan should now look like that shown in Figure 3.36.

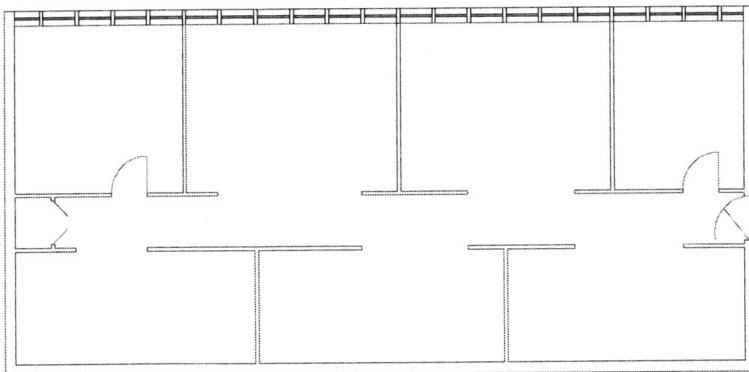

Figure 3.36 The plan so far.

Making Repeatable Symbols

If you have an object in a drawing that appears more than once, it is possible to make a 'copy' of that object and place it elsewhere in the drawing. This is done with the *Construct/Block* command, which turns separate and diverse objects into a single symbol or block as it is called in AutoCAD LT. The newly created block can be placed in the drawing with the *Draw/Insert Block* command. Unlike *Modify/ Copy* the *Insert* command allows us to scale in both X and Y directions and rotate the block through 360°.

Basic Rules for Blocks

Insertion points are standardly placed in the lower left-hand corner of the block, except where block usage would dictate otherwise. Rectangular or square blocks would follow this convention, but a circular block would normally have the insertion point at its centre. What is an insertion point?

When a block is created it needs a 'hook' or insertion point. This is the point on the block that is attached to the cursor when you insert the block back into your drawing.

Blocks made on layer 0 have a special adaptive quality. Whatever layer the block is inserted on, it adopts the colour and linetype of that layer. Blocks made on other layers retain the properties of the layer on which they were made.

A block can be updated, or redefined as AutoCAD LT calls it, by redrawing the block and naming it with the same name as a previous block. Once that block is redefined all occurrences of that block in the drawing are updated to the new block and the old definition no longer exists. We will use the *Block* and *Insert* commands to create and place the furniture in the plan.

Use *Settings/LayerControl* and make Layer 0 the current layer. *View/Zoom/Window* to a blank area of the drawing. We will construct a block by practising on the coffee table to get you started.

To Create a Block

Turn the grid and snap on if they aren't already (F7 and F9). Refer to Figure 3.40 for the dimensions of the coffee table. Use *Draw/Line* and draw the coffee table using the grid and snap. To convert it into a block use *Construct/Make Block* and a dialogue box will appear as shown in Figure 3.37. Type the block name at the flashing cursor (coftabl). Next, choose the block insertion point by clicking on *Select Point*. After the dialogue box disappears click on the bottom left-hand corner of the coffee table as shown in Figure 3.38. If you have used grid and snap the cursor will automatically position itself at this corner.

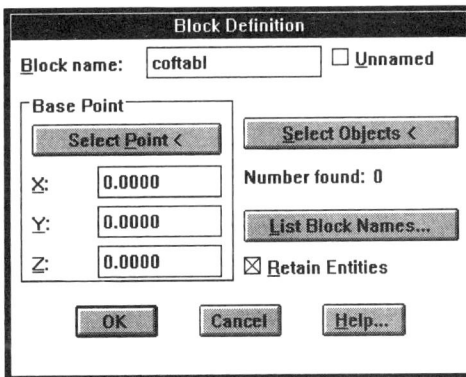

Figure 3.37   Block Definition dialogue box.

Figure 3.38   Creating a block.

The dialogue box will reappear. Now click on the *Select Objects* button and the dialogue box disappears again to enable you to choose the objects to turn into a block (the four lines forming the coffee table). Pick the four lines and the dialogue box reappears again. If the *Retain Entities* box is checked when you click on *OK* the coffee table will remain on screen, otherwise it will disappear. The block is now made.

To Insert a Block

To insert a block into the drawing use *Draw/Insert Block* and a dialogue box will appear.

Click on Block... and another dialogue box will overlay the previous one as shown in Figure 3.39. Click on Coftabl and *OK* it and *OK* again in the first dialogue box. The dialogue will disappear to show

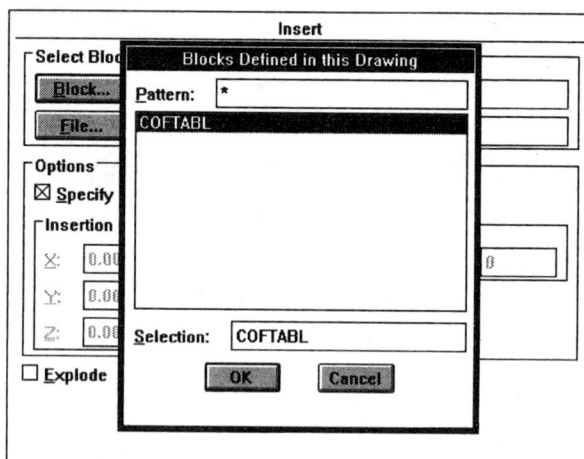

Figure 3.39 Insert Block dialogue box.

the cursor attached to the bottom left-hand corner of the block – the insertion point that you chose earlier. You can now select a position in the drawing. The command line will appear as shown below. Press Return for X and Y scale factors and the rotation angle.

```
Insertion point: pick a point on the drawing
X scale factor<1>/Corner/XYZ: Return
Yscale factor: Return
Rotation angle<0.000>: Return
```

Insert the coffee table once again but change the X scale factor to 2 and the Y scale factor to 0.5 with a 45° rotation angle. Can you see what has happened? You have stretched the coffee table by a factor of 2 in the X direction, by 0.5 in the Y direction and rotated it through 45°. Erase these two blocks and when selected you will see that they are no longer separate lines but one object.

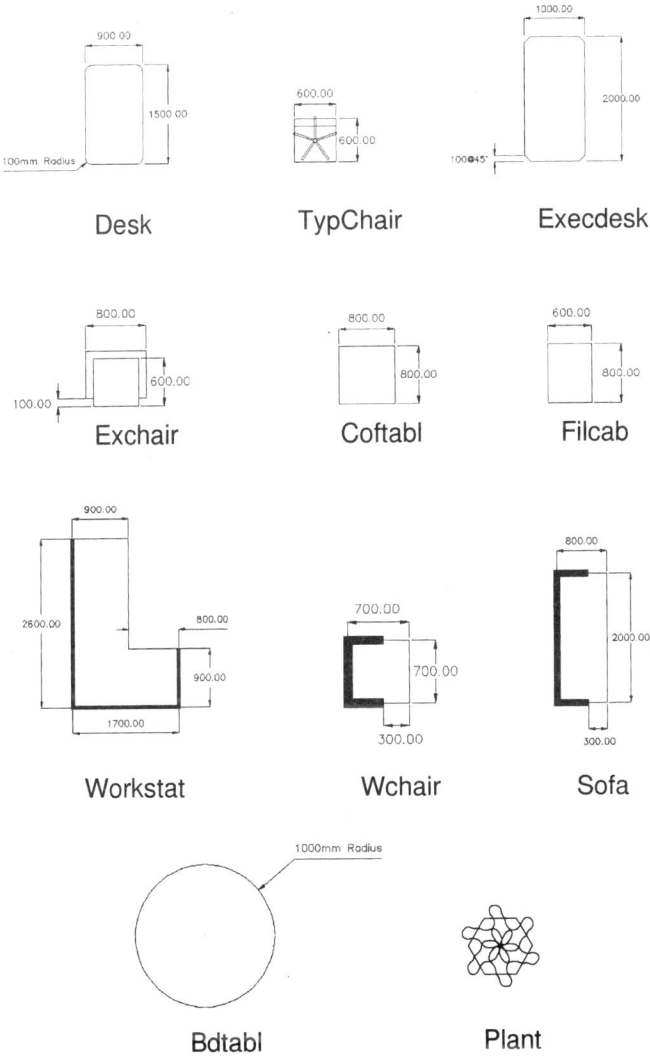

Figure 3.40 The dimensions and shapes of the blocks.

You are now ready to create the remainder of the blocks. Specific drawing instructions follow for constructing each block. Refer to Figure 3.40 for the dimensions of the blocks.

The Execdesk Block
The Chamfer Command

The *Chamfer* command produces bevelled corners. If the chamfer distances are set to 0, the lines will be automatically trimmed or extended to meet each other as discussed in more depth in Chapter 4. We will use Chamfer to produce the bevelled corners on the Execdesk block. First, draw the outline of the desk in a rectangular shape. Before chamfering the corners we have to set the chamfer distances as shown in Figure 3.41.

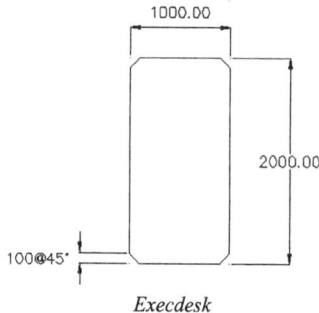

Execdesk

Figure 3.41   The Execdesk block.

Use *Modify/Chamfer:*

> *Polyline/Distances/<Select first line>:* **D**
> *Enter first camfer distance<0.00>:* **100**
> *Enter second chamfer distance<100.00>:* **100**

Re-activate the command:

> *Polyline/Distances/<Select first line>:* **pick** *one line*
> *Select second line:* **pick** *its adjoining line*

Complete the other corners and make a block of it.

The Desk Block
The Fillet Command
The *Fillet* command draws a user-specified curve between two lines. If the fillet radius is set to 0, the lines will be automatically trimmed or extended to meet each other. We will use *Fillet* to produce radii on the corners of the Desk block. Similar to the *Chamfer* command, we have to set a radius before filleting the corners as shown in Figure 3.42.

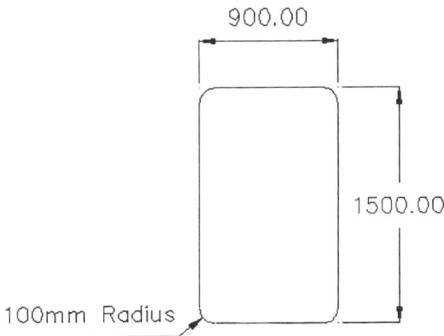

Figure 3.42 The Desk block.

Use *Modify/Fillet:*

> *Polyline/Radius/<select first object>:* **R**
> *Enter fillet radius<0.00>:* **100**

Re-activate the command:

> *Polyline/Radius/<select first object>:* **pick** *one line*
> *Select second object:* **pick** *its adjoining line*

Complete the other corners and block it.

The Workstat, Wchair and Sofa Blocks
The Polyline Command

A pline or polyline can be a line segment, an arc, or a combination of both. It can have a uniform or varying width. When a pline is drawn as connected segements, it acts as a single object. We will use pline to draw the backs of the Workstat, Wchair and Sofa blocks as shown in Figure 3.43. Draw the outlines of the objects first with *Line*. After picking its start point, the starting and ending widths of the polyline have to be stated.

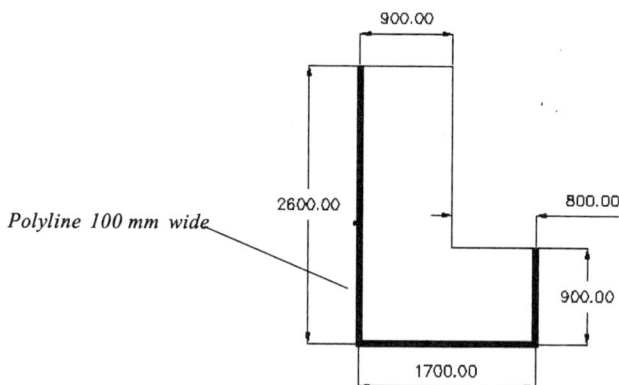

Figure 3.43   The Workstat block showing the polylines.

Use *Draw/Polyline:*

> From point: **pick** its start point on the object
> Arc/Close/Halfwidth/Length/Undo/Width/<Endpoint of line>: **W**
> Starting width<0.00>: **100**
> Ending width<100.00>: **100**
> Arc/close/Halfwidth/Length/Undo/Width/<Endpoint of line>: **pick** the corners on the object

The Typist Chair
The Circle Command
Object Snap – QUADrant
Point Filters
The Array/Polar command

The drawing of the typist chair contains a number of useful features that we can utilize. The central pillar is a circle, and we can position this circle in the centre of the square with Point Filters. The legs can be drawn with a polyline and polar arrayed around the circle to complete the chair. The start point of the leg can be started at the quadrant point of the circle.

Point filters are not a command, but a way of constructing a point by giving x, y, and z coordinates separately instead of all at once. We have already used the *Array* command for the windows, but this time we will use the polar option to copy the legs around a central point. Use *Draw/Line* to complete the outline of the chair and its backrest. As shown in Figure 3.44, to draw the central pillar use *Draw/Circle/Cen Rad:*

> *Circle/3P/2P/TTR/<Center point>: .X* **(type a dot and X)** *of* **MIDpoint** *of the edge as shown*
> *of(need YZ): .Y* **(type a dot and Y)** *of* **MIDpoint** *of the edge as shown*
> *of(need Z):* **0**
> *Diameter/<Radius>: Drag* **25**

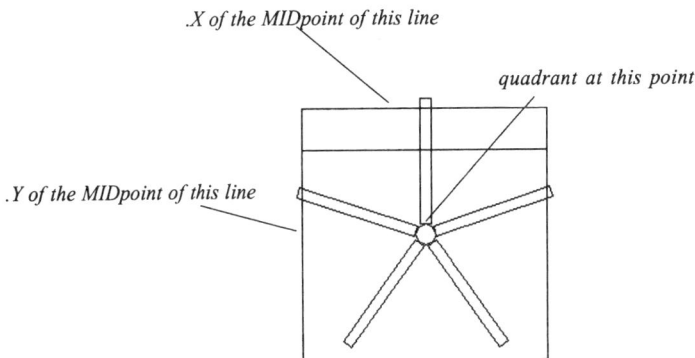

.X of the MIDpoint of this line

quadrant at this point

.Y of the MIDpoint of this line

Figure 3.44   The Typist chair using point filters and Object snap — quadrant.

Before drawing set the polyline width back to 0. It will also help to make the chair outline as large as possible, so zoom it up. To draw a chair leg, use *Draw/Polyline:*

> *From point:* **pick** *its start point on the object*
> *Arc/Close/Halfwidth/Length/Undo/Width/<Endpoint of line>:* **W**

From point: **pick** *its start point on the object*
Arc/Close/Halfwidth/Length/Undo/Width/<Endpoint of line>: **W**
Starting width<0.00>: **100**
Ending width<100.00>: **100** *Endpoint of line: QUADrant* **pick** *the 12*
o'clock point on the circle
Endpoint of line: **@12.5<180**
Endpoint of line: **@300<90**
Endpoint of line: **@25<0**
Endpoint of line: **@300<270**
Endpoint of line: **@12.5<180**

Modify/Array/Polar the leg around the centre of the circle and answer *Y* to rotate objects as they are copied. Block the object when finished.

The Plant Block
The Polygon Command
To draw the plant container we are going to use the Polygon command to draw a six-sided pot and the polyline command to draw the plant as shown in Figure 3.45. We will then Block the drawing with the block insertion point at approximately the centre of the polygon. Use the pull-down menu *Draw/Polygon:*

Command: _polygon
Number of Sides<default>: **6**
Edge/<Center of polygon>: **pick** *a point*
Radius of circle: **500**

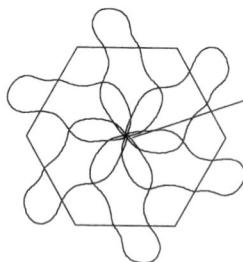

approximate centre of
polygon –
centre of array and
insertion point
of block

Figure 3.45   The plant block.

To draw the leaves of the plant use *Draw/Polyline* and draw just one leaf of the plant. Use *Modify/Edit Polyline* to smooth the curve with *F* for fit and then exit the command.

Select Polyline: **pick** *the leaf*
Close/Join/Width/Edit Vertex/Fit/Spline curve/Decurve/Ltype gen/Undo/
eXit<x> **F**
Close/Join/Width/Edit Vertex/Fit/Spline curve/Decurve/Ltype gen/Undo/
eXit<x> **X**

Use *Array/Polar* to revolve the leaf six times around the approximate centre of the polygon as shown in Figure 3.45.

The Filing Cabinet Block
Complete the filing cabinet in the same way as the coffee table but try altering the grid and snap values so that you have a rectangular grid to coincide with the shape of the filing cabinet.

The Board Table
Use *Draw/Circle* with a radius of 1000 and the insertion point of the block at the centre of the circle.

Inserting the Blocks into the Drawing
Before inserting the blocks remember that we need to insert them onto the layers that we made earlier – the desk types and table on the Desk layer, the chairs and sofa on the Chair layer, etc. Choose your own layer name and colour on which to insert the plant. Use *Settings/Layer Control* and make each relevant layer current.

Insert the blocks onto their layer. You should see the blocks adopt the colour of the layer as described earlier.

Making Layers Invisible
The purpose of layering is to allow what would have been multiple drawings in manual drafting to appear on one single drawing in AutoCAD LT. Making layers visible and invisible is done via the *Freeze* and *Thaw* buttons in the Layer Dialogue box as shown in Figure 3.46. After highlighting a layer name the 'greyed out' buttons become active. Use *Freeze* to make the selected layer or layers invisible. Remember that invisible layers are not printed.

Freeze all the layers on which you have placed the blocks. Remember that you cannot freeze the current layer.

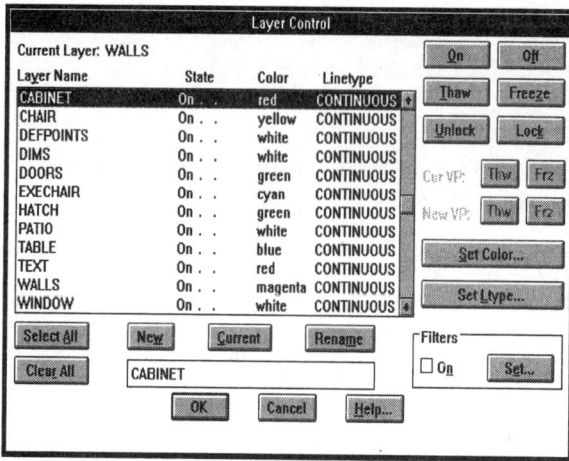

Figure 3.46   Layer Control dialogue box with layer selected and buttons active.

Drawing the Patio Edge
The PolyArc Command
The Hatch Command

The *Hatch* command allows us to place a stored hatch pattern into the drawing. We are going to hatch the patio area, excluding the pond. However, before we do that, we have to draw a boundary and

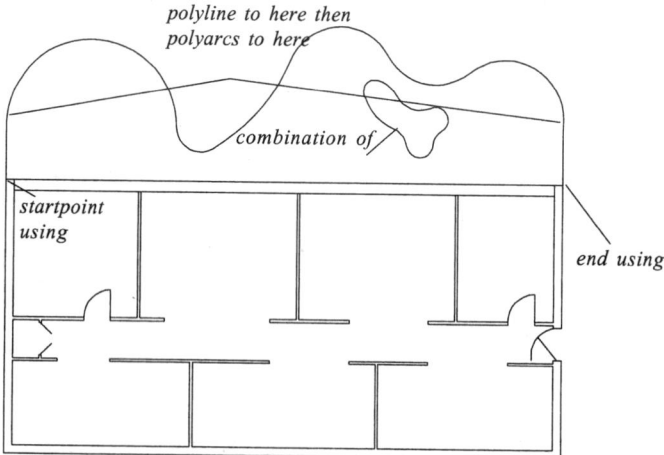

Figure 3.47   The edge of the patio.

we will use a combination of the *Polyline* and *PolyArc* options as shown in Figure 3.47. Remember that to hatch we must have a closed boundary, i.e. no gaps. Use *Draw/Polyline:*

From point: **pick** *the intersection as shown*
Arc/Close/Halfwidth/Length/Undo/Width/<Endpoint of line>: **W**
Starting width<100>: **1**
Ending width<1>: **1**
Arc/Close/Halfwidth/Length/Undo/Width/<Endpoint of line>: **pick** *as shown*
Arc/Close/Halfwidth/Length/Undo/Width/<Endpoint of line>: **A** *(for Arc)*
Arc/Close/Halfwidth/Length/Undo/Width/<Endpoint of arc>: **pick** *arc shapes and directions to suit*
Arc/Close/Halfwidth/Length/Undo/Width/<Endpoint of arc>: **L** *(for line – to return to line shape)*
Arc/Close/Halfwidth/Length/Undo/Width/<Endpoint of arc>: **pick** *the intersection*

Use *Settings/Layer Control*, make a new layer called Hatch, and set it to Current. Click *OK*.

Use *Draw/BoundaryHatch*, then click on *Pattern*. Click on a pattern suitable for a patio as shown in Figure 3.48.

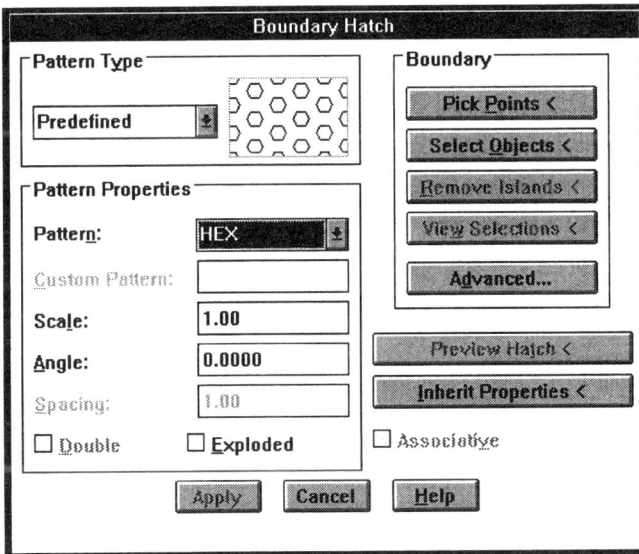

Figure 3.48   The Boundary Hatch dialogue box.

The chosen name will appear alongside the *Pattern...* button. Click *OK*. Click on *Select Objects* and then select the polyline outline of the patio, the outer wall of the building and lastly the pond.

Use *Preview Hatch* to look at the hatched area and *Apply* if you are satisfied. If you want to alter the scale of the pattern select Pattern... again and enter a suitable scale.

Annotating the Drawing (Entering Text)

AutoCAD LT provides us with many ways in which to add text to drawings and many text styles called fonts. You can also change the existing styles by angling, compressing and stretching the characters. The command Draw/Text is used to enter text. Dynamic text has the feature of placing a square box in lieu of the next character and indicates the location as you enter it. Before we enter text we must choose the style but you only have to do this once.

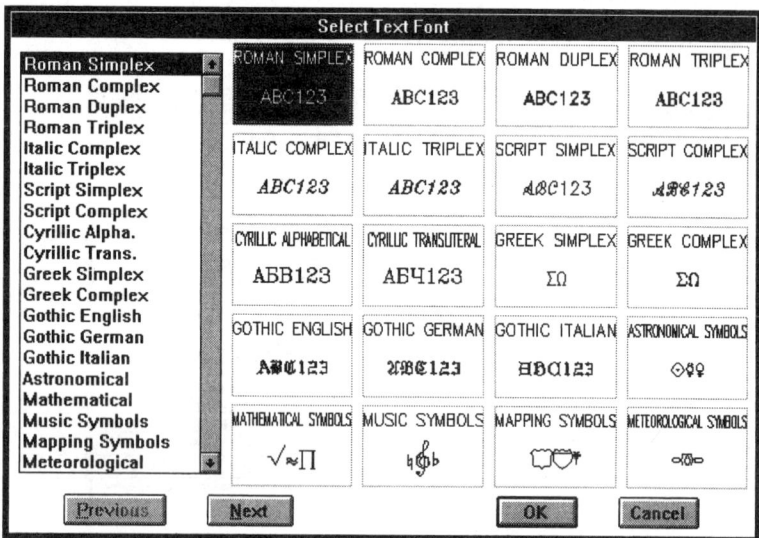

Figure 3.49 The Select Text Font dialogue box.

Use the pull-down menu *Settings/Text Style*. Click in the Roman Simplex style and then *OK* it as shown in Figure 3.49.

font file<txt>: romans Height <0.000>: **Return**
Width factor <1>: **Return** *(the text can be stretched by entering figures >1)*
Obliquing angle <0>: **Return** *(e.g. The text can be made italic by entering15°)*
Backwards <N>: **Return**
Upside Down <N>: **Return**
Vertical <N>: **Return**
Romans is now the current style

Refer to the target drawing, Figure 3.6, and enter the required text using *Draw/Text.* Below is an example of entering the text 'Chief Executive'.

Command:_dtext Justify/Style/<Start point>: c (for the bottom centre of the words)
center point: **pick**
Height: <3.00>: **100**
Rotation angle <0>: **Return**
Text: **Chief** *(***Return** *once)*
Text: **Executive** *(***Return** *twice)*

Adding Dimensions to the Drawing

AutoCAD LT allows us to dimension objects in a drawing accurately with the *Draw/Dimensions* command. This can take the form of linear dimensions, horizontal, vertical, aligned and rotated. You can chain dimensions together with *Continue* or measure from a common baseline. Ordinate dimensions measure the perpendicular distance from an origin point. Radial dimensions give a radius or diameter of a circle or arc with or without a centre mark. Angular dimensions measure the angle between two lines or three points. Lastly, you can add a note called a leader which is an arrow with a line attached with any text you wish to accompany it.

A whole range of dimension styles is available and can be altered with *Settings/Dimension Style.* We will use this pull-down to produce the dimensions shown in Figure 3.54. Use the pull down and a dialogue box appears as shown in Figure 3.50.

Select the *Arrows...* button and change to the arrow style with a size of 100 as shown in Figure 3.51. Click on *OK* and select *Text Location...* and change the size of the text height to 125. *In the Horizontal* box change to *Force Text Inside* which forces the text to be

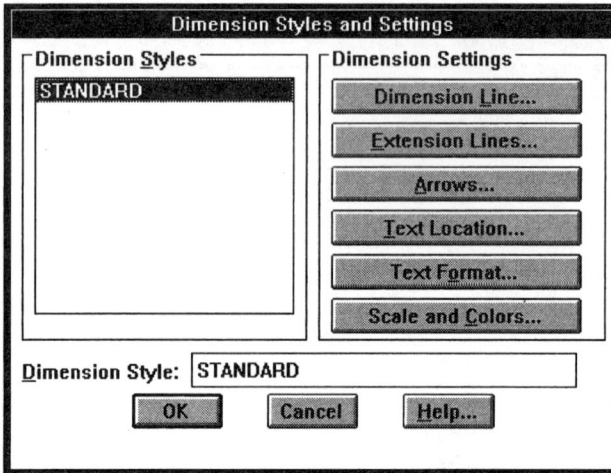

Figure 3.50   The Dimension Styles and Settings dialogue box.

placed inside the dimension arrows. In the *Vertical* box, change the
value to *Above* which will place the text above the dimension line
and in the *Alignment* box change to *Align with Dimension Line* as
shown in Figure 3.52. *OK* that and activate the *Extension Lines*
dialogue box to change the *Extension Above Line* to 50 which is the

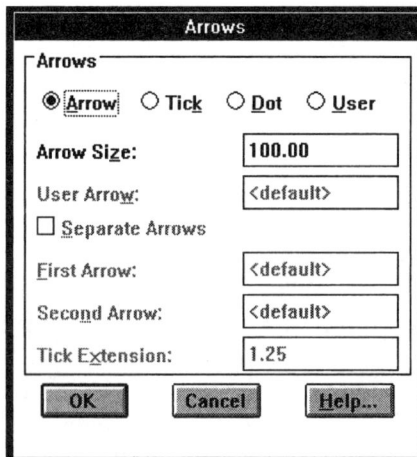

Figure 3.51   The Arrows dialogue box.

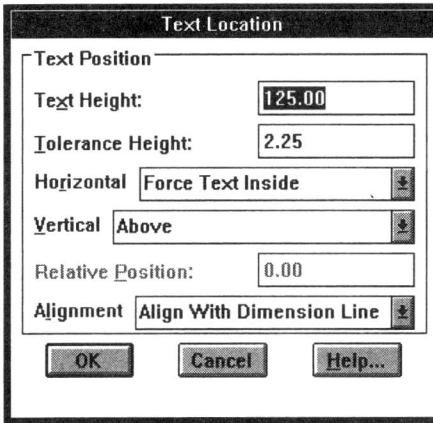

Figure 3.52 Text Location dialogue box.

length of the extension line protruding above the arrow end. Change *Feature Offset* to 100 which is the gap between the end of the extension line and the object you have measured. The *Visibility* of the extension lines should be set at *Draw Both* as shown in Figure 3.53.

You have created certain parameters for your dimensions and if you want to use them again it is wise to save them with a meaningful name. In this way it is possible to have different dimensioning styles

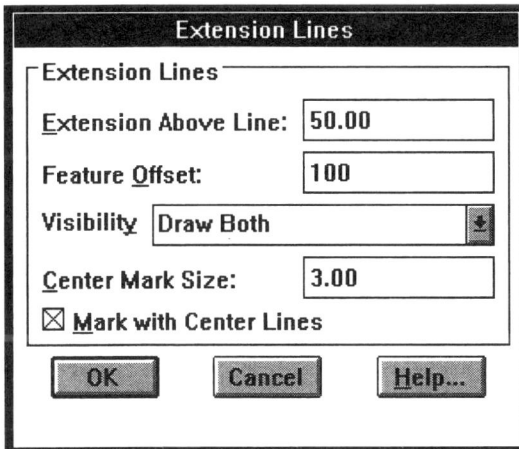

Figure 3.53 Extension Lines dialogue box.

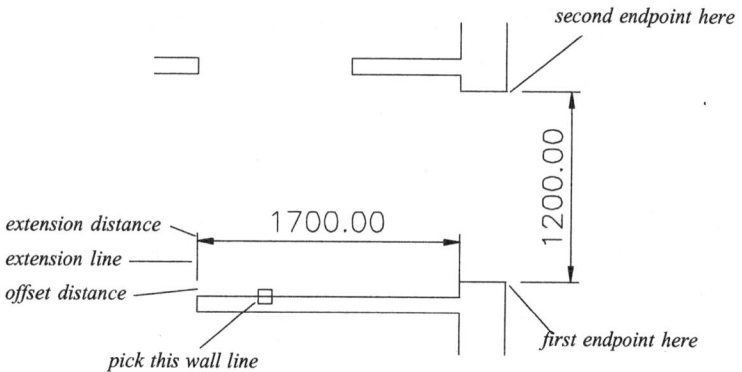

Figure 3.54   Horizontal and vertical dimensioning.

within the same drawing. Remember that when a style is loaded it defaults to that style until deliberately changed. To save a style simply type the name at the *Dimension Style* as shown in Figure 3.50. We have used the name *Standard*, which, when saved, appears as a named style in the list in that dialogue box.

Make the Dimensions layer current. As shown in Figure 3.54 we will dimension the right-hand side doorway and adjacent wall. To dimension the wall which measures 1700.00 use the pull-down menu *Draw/ Dimensions/Linear/Horizontal:*

> *First extension line origin or RETURN to select:* **Return**
> *Select line, arc or circle:* **pick** *the wall as shown*
> *Dimension line location:* **pick** *a point above the wall*
> *Dimension text <1700.00>:* **Return**
> *Dim:* **Return**

and the length of the wall is dimensioned. To dimension the doorway which measures 1200.00 use *Draw/Dimension/Linear/Vertical.* For this we cannot press Return as the first response as the distance to be measured is not an object so we will use Object snap – ENDpoint to locate the openings. (You could, instead, turn *Snap* on (F9) as the endpoints coincide with the grid and snap on our original settings.)

> *First extension line origin or RETURN to select:* **end**point *(or intersection)*
> *of* **pick** *one end of the doorway as shown*
> *Second extension line origin:* **end**
> *of* **pick** *the opposite end of the doorway as shown*
> *Dimension line location:* **pick** *a point opposite the doorway*

*Dimension text <1200.00>: **Return***
*Dim: **Exit***

Practise with the different settings by dimensioning other parts of the drawing.

Adding a Third Dimension (3D)

Converting a drawing from 2D to 3D is a simple process. In our example we will convert the walls and windows of the building from a zero height to 2600 with the *Change Properties* command. Height in AutoCAD LT is expressed as Thickness. *Freeze* all the layers except Walls and Windows and use the pull-down menu *Modify/ Change Properties:*

*Select objects: **put** a window around the drawing*
*Select objects: **Return***

After the dialogue box appears enter the new *Thickness* of 2600 and click *OK* as shown Figure 3.55.

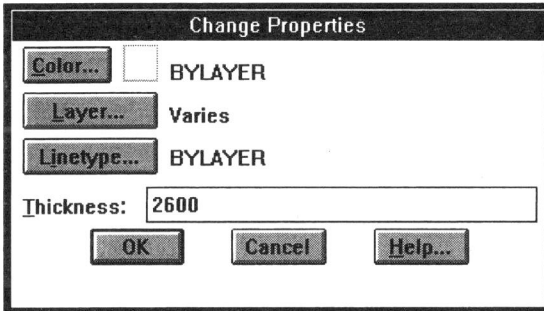

Figure 3.55 The Change Properties dialogue box.

Looking at the Drawing in 3D

You will not have noticed a difference in your drawing yet as it is still in the plan view, i.e. looking directly down. To view the drawing in 3D we will need to change our view from above to a more oblique viewpoint, but first, *Thaw* the *Patioedge* and *Hatch* layers.

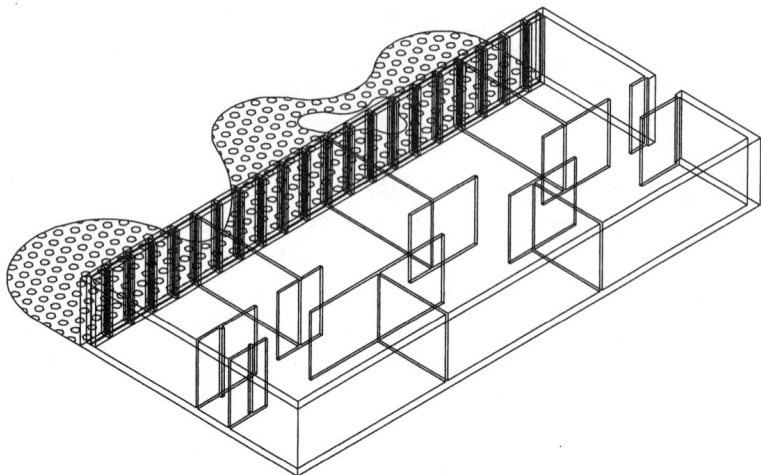

Figure 3.56   The 3D view of the target drawing.

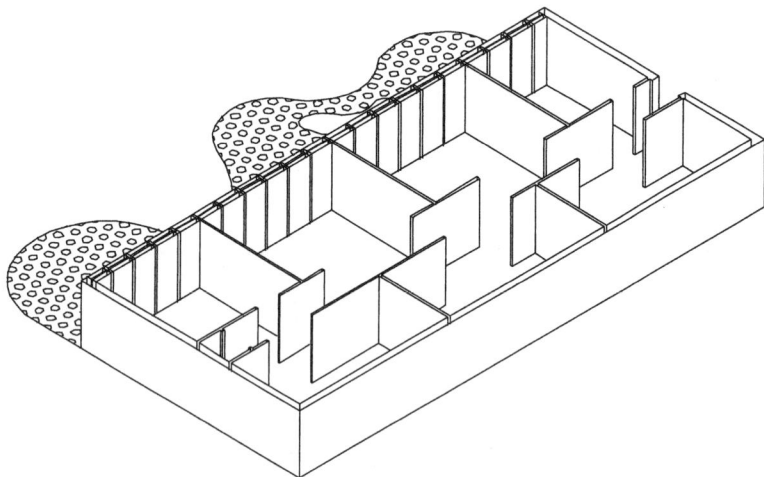

Figure 3.57   The 3D view of the target drawing after Hide.

Use the pull-down menu *View/Set View/3D Viewpoint Presets/Iso View SW* and the target drawing will appear as shown in Figure 3.56. It appears as a 'see through' model. Use *View/Hide* and the model becomes solid as shown in Figure 3.57.

Remember that you cannot convert the blocks into 3D unless you explode them, apply thicknesses and re-block them.

Looking at Different Views
The viewpoint shown in Figure 3.57 is a parallel projection, i.e. it is non-perspective. To look at the model with a perspective view we can use the *View/3D Dynamic View* command but before that we need to return to a plan view of the model. Use *View/3D Plan View/ World UCS* to return and you should now have a plan view on screen. Activate the *3D Dynamic View:*

> *Select objects:* **put** *a window around the drawing*
> *Select objects:* **Return**
> *Camera/TArget/Distance/POints/PAn/Zoom/TWist/CLip/ Hide/Off/Undo/*
> *<eXit>:* **d**
> *New camera/target distance<1.00>:* **40000**
> *Camera/TArget/Distance/POints/PAn/Zoom/TWist/CLip/ Hide/Off/Undo/*
> *<eXit>:* **h**

The model should now be as shown in Figure 3.58. Save the view of this drawing with *View/View/Save:*

> '_view/Delete/Restore/Save/Window: **S**
> *View name to save:* **1**

Reactivate the command (press the spacebar or Return) and we will produce another view using the *CAmera* option. The model will 'disappear' and as you move your cursor around the screen it regenerates itself. As a rule of thumb, the top central position of the screen is virtually a plan view, the centre middle screen is a side-on view and the bottom middle is a view from underneath.

> *Camera/TArget/Distance/POints/PAn/Zoom/TWist/CLip/ Hide/Off/Undo/*
> *<eXit>:* **ca**
> *New camera/target distance<1.00>:* **pick** *a point on screen*
> *Camera/TArget/Distance/POints/PAn/Zoom/TWist/CLip/ Hide/Off/Undo/*
> *<eXit>:* **h**
> *Camera/TArget/Distance/POints/PAn/Zoom/TWist/CLip/ Hide/Off/Undo/*
> *<eXit>:* **x**

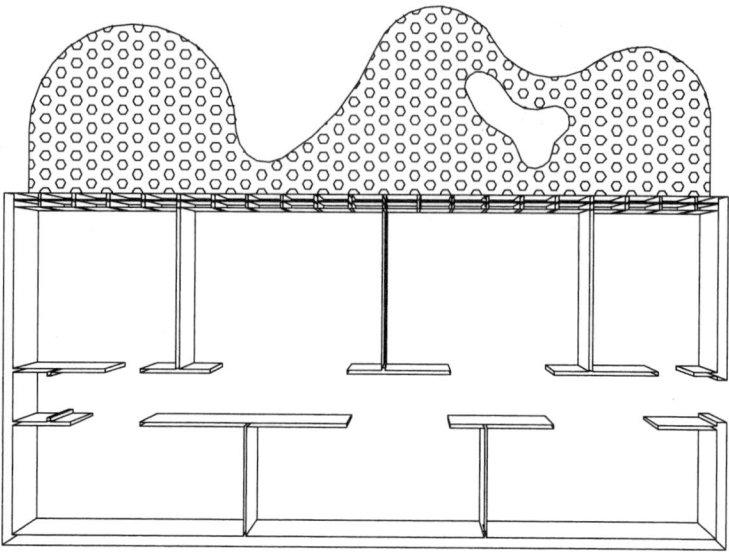

Figure 3.58   The 3D Dynamic view command with Distance and Hide.

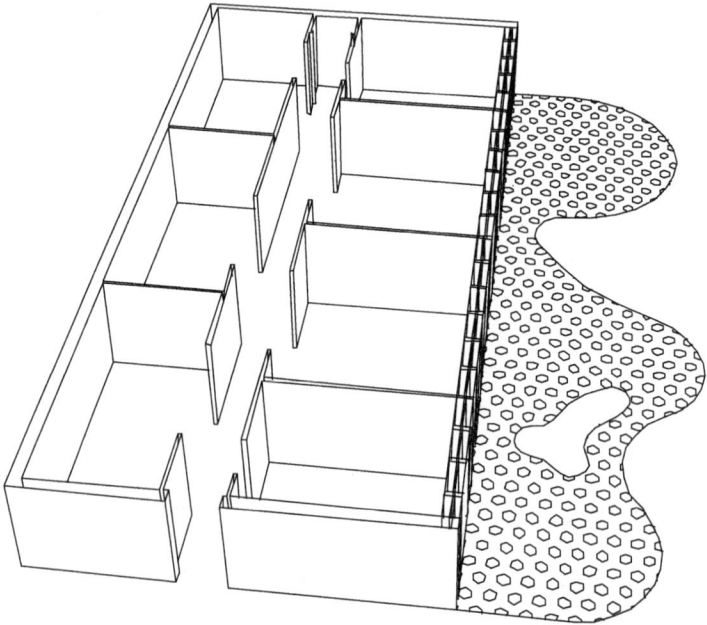

Figure 3.59   The 3D Dynamic view command with Camera and Hide.

Figure 3.59 shows a view of the model after using the *CAmera* and *Hide* options. Save this view with the name '2'.

Paper Space and Model Space

So far, when you have been creating your model you have been working in what is known as Model Space. You can split the screen into tiled viewports, i.e. you can display different views of the drawing or model adjacent to each other in the same view on screen as shown in Figure 3.60.

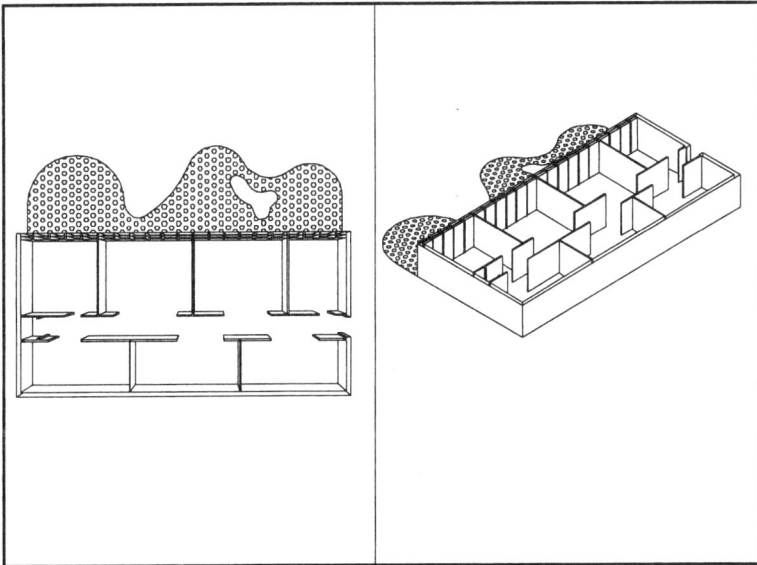

Figure 3.60 Tile viewports in Model Space.

Paper Space is the area which represents the 'drawing sheet' on which the overall layout of the drawing takes place prior to plotting. Paper Space differs from Model Space in that any objects drawn in Paper Space are plotted at a 1:1 ratio. Put simply, if you want 5 mm high text in Model Space you must take account of the final plotted scale of the drawing. In Paper Space, if 5 mm high text is required, 5 mm text is selected.

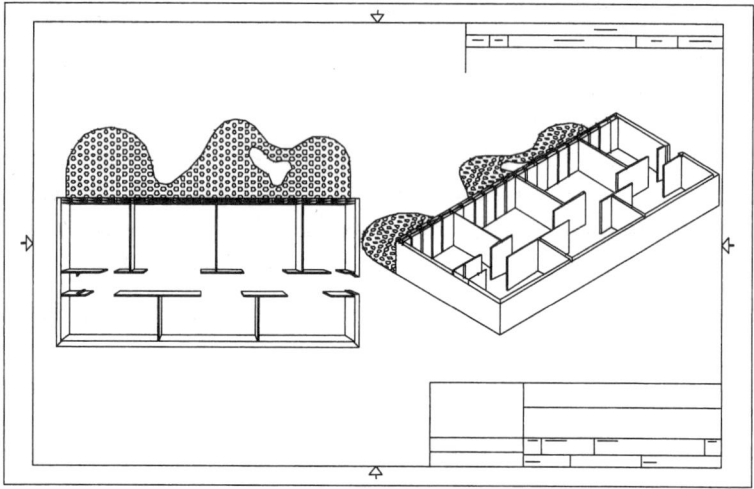

Figure 3.61   Paper Space with two views of the drawing and border.

In our next exercise we will set up two viewports as shown in Figure 3.60, switch to Paper Space, set up two viewports, import the drawing from Model Space and insert a pre-drawn border as shown in Figure 3.61.

Create two layers, *Psvports* and *Border*. Make Psvports *Current* with a prominent colour (try red).

First, let's set up the two viewports in Model Space. Go back to a plan view of the drawing with *View/3D Plan View/World UCS*. Then use *View/Viewports* and you will see the plan view repeated in both viewports as shown in Figure 3.62.

*Save/Restore/Delete/Join/SIngle/?/2/<3>/4: **2***

The command *Tilemode* controls access to Paper Space and is typed at the command line as *TM*.

*Command: **TM***
*New value for Tilemode <1>: **0***

Your drawing will disappear and in the bottom left corner of the screen a Paper Space icon will replace the WCS (World Coordinate System) icon which is shown in Figure 3.63.

Use *View/Viewport/2 Viewports* to generate two Paper Space viewports:

Horizontal/<Vertical>: **Return** *(accept the default)*
Fit/<first point>: **F**

'F' fits the two viewports within the screen view. You will now have a view similar to that shown in Figure 3.62 but with the Paper Space icon in the bottom left corner of the screen. You are now in Paper Space − try to erase any of the objects in the drawing. If you do,

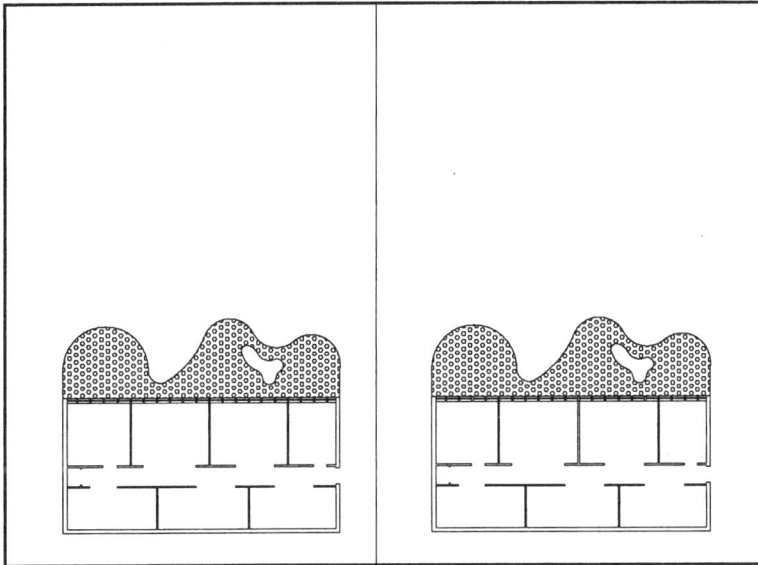

Figure 3.62 Tiled viewports in Model space, plan view.

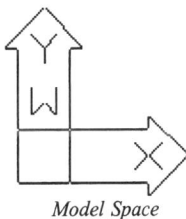

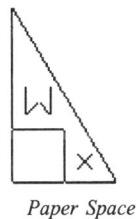

Model Space   *Paper Space*

Figure 3.63 Model Space and Paper Space icons.

AutoCAD LT will tell you that none was found. That's because they don't exist in Paper Space. Only the red borders do. Move the cursor around the screen and you will see that it's not constricted within the boundaries of the viewports – it roams around the screen 'over' the viewports.

At the command line type *MS* for Model Space. We have reverted to Model Space. Note how the cursor is now restricted to the viewport boundaries and when it moves from one viewport to another it changes to a pointer – the inactive viewport. Click on the pick button and it becomes active. Recall the previously saved views with *View/View/ Restore* and restore views 1 and 2 in each viewport.

> '_view/Delete/Restore/Save/Window: *R*
> *View name to restore: 1*

Use *View/Hide* to 'solidify' the model in both viewports. You will have to repeat the command for each active viewport. Return to Paper Space by typing *PS* at the command line.

Inserting The Border
We are now ready to insert one of the pre-drawn ANSII borders that come supplied with AutoCAD LT. Make the layer Border current. Use *Draw/Insert Block* and click the *File...* button to insert an external drawing file. Choose a suitable ANSI_ drawing border as shown in Figure 3.64. The border shown in Figure 3.61 is ANSI_C.

> *Insertion point: 0,0*
> *X scale factor<1>/Corner/XYZ: Return*
> *Yscale factor: Return*
> *Rotation angle<0.000>: Return*

You will probably find that the border overlaps the two views of the model. Pick the viewport border (the red outline) and move them both individually so that they sit neatly in the drawing and inside the inserted border. *Freeze* the *Psvports* layer. Your drawing should now look like Figure 3.61. *Zoom* into the text box of the inserted border and add your name and other pertinent details.

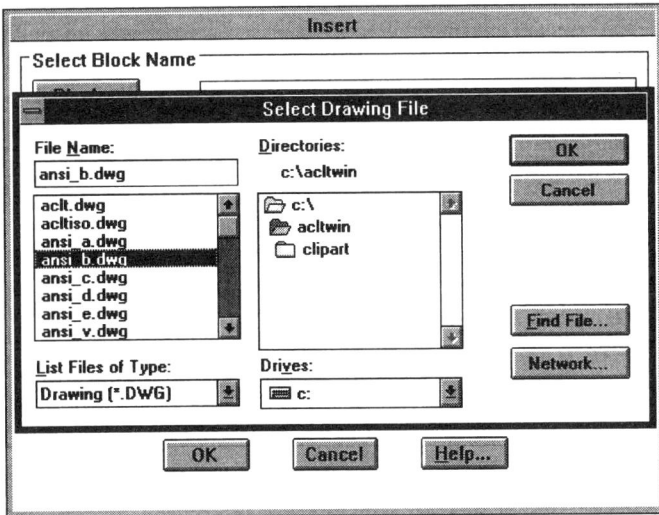

Figure 3.64 The Insert Block external file option.

Plotting from Model Space

If you are plotting a 3D model from Paper Space you only need to remember to use the *View/Viewports/Hideplot* command. This ensures that the drawing appears 'solidified' when plotted rather than see through. You will have to *Thaw* the *Psvports* layer and re-freeze before plotting.

    ON/OFF/Hideplot/Fit/2/3/4/Restore/<First Point>_hideplot ON/OFF: **On**
    Select objects: **pick** both the viewport borders (the red rectangles)

Remember that picking the drawing detail is pointless as it does not exist in Paper Space – only the borders do. You are now ready to plot the drawing. Refer to Chapter 5 where it is covered in depth.

4 Editing your Drawings

Next to drawing you will spend most of your time editing, changing and amending your drawings. A good CAD drawing is generally the result of attention to detail which owes as much to efficiency in drawing as it does to your editing skills.

The Two Ways to Edit in AutoCAD LT

In the command-oriented approach you issue a command such as *Erase* to start the amending process. AutoCAD LT then invites you to select the objects to be erased as shown in Figure 4.1. Remember that you can also type the commands at the keyboard and the response is just the same.

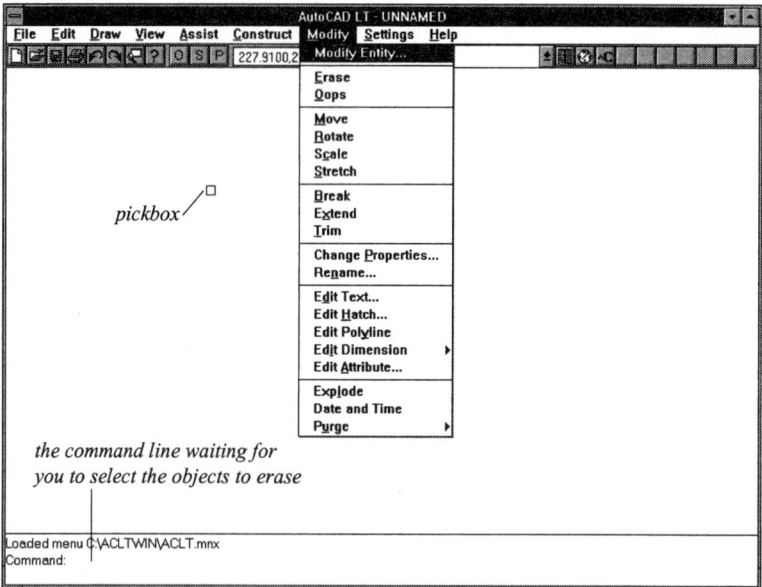

Figure 4.1 The drawing editor showing the Modify pop-down and the command line response.

The second approach is the opposite of the first where you select the object to be edited and then issue the command. When this method is used a series of small boxes appear at points on the object. These boxes are called grips and they are manipulated by selecting them. Figure 4.2 shows lines that have been selected with grips appearing at the endpoints and midpoints. Grips can be disabled by typing the *Grips* command at the command line and setting that system variable to 0 as shown in Figure 4.3.

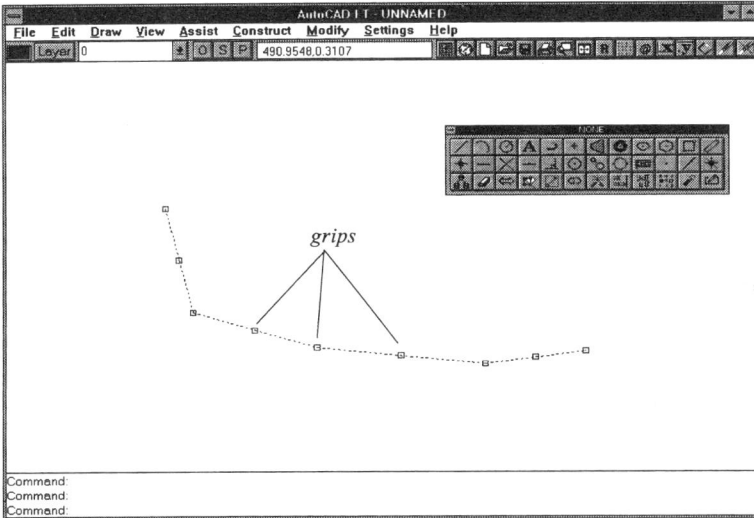

Figure 4.2 Grip selection.

```
Command: grips
New value for GRIPS <1>: 0
Command:
```

Figure 4.3 Disabling grips.

Changing the Size of the Pickbox

Before we look at the methods of selecting objects you will have seen in Figure 4.1 a reference to a 'pickbox'. The pickbox replaces the cursor when you issue one of the editing commands. The pickbox size can be changed by using the *Settings/Selection Style* pull-down. A dialogue box appears as shown in Figure 4.4. The pickbox size is changed via the slider bar and you will probably find that you need to change this during an editing session.

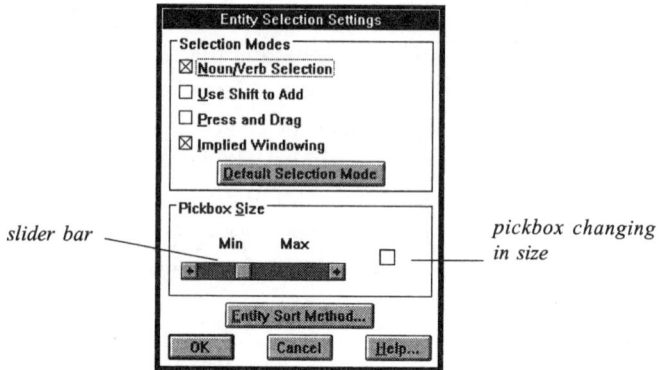

Figure 4.4   The Entity Selection Settings dialogue box.

Selecting Individual Objects for Editing

In AutoCAD LT you can select objects for editing individually and in groups. By selecting individually you simply press the left mouse button once with the pickbox over the object. If you use the first method of selection as described in the section on 'Two ways to edit' you issue the command first and then continue picking until the selection set is complete. You then press Return and, if you used the *Erase*

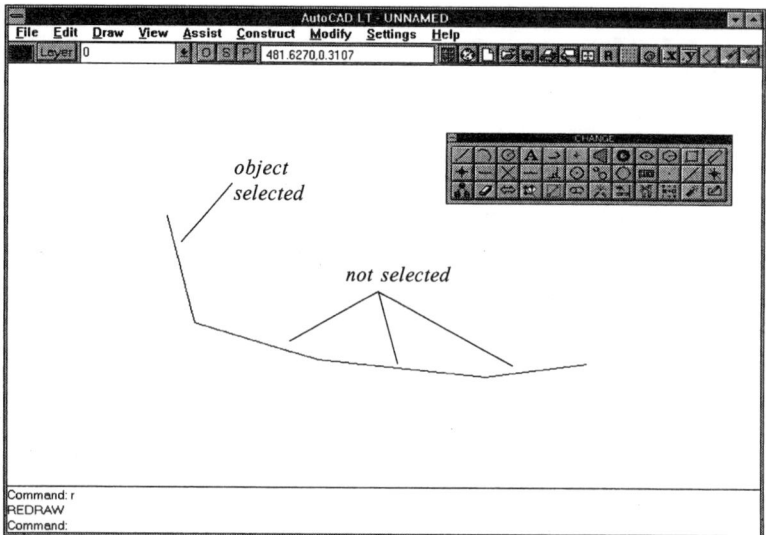

Figure 4.5   Object selection before and after picking.

command, for instance, all the objects disappear. As you are picking each object it converts to a dotted appearance indicating that it has been chosen, as shown in Figure 4.5.

Selecting Groups of Objects for Editing

Selecting a group of objects for editing is achieved in one of three ways:

Placing a rectangular window around the objects or

An irregularly shaped window or

A line (called a fence) passing through the objects

although any combination of these can be used in one selection set. In addition, the window can be made to select only those objects that are totally contained within the selection window, or objects that are not only totally contained within the selection window but any objects that pass through or touch any part of the window. To select objects contained only within the window, you drag the cursor from left to right. This creates a *window* selection with a solid outline. If you drag your cursor from right to left it creates a *crossing* window and, as the name suggests, any object crossing through the window boundary is selected. A crossing window is differentiated from a selection window by its broken line appearance as shown in Figure 4.6. If you look at the selection window in Figure 4.6 only one object is selected because it is the only one that is fully enclosed by the window.

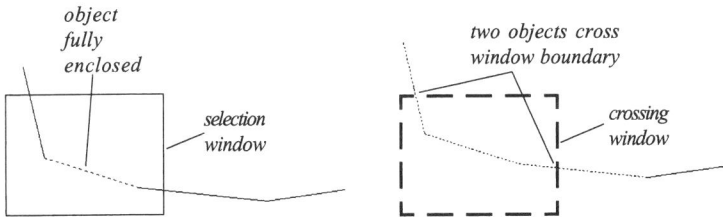

Figure 4.6 Selection by window and crossing window.

In contrast the crossing window selects three objects even though only one is fully enclosed. This is because the two other objects are crossing through the window boundary. Extreme care must be used with a crossing window as objects can be selected when not intended. If you do inadvertently select an object you can deselect it by typing '*r*' for remove at the command line as shown in Figure 4.7. Once you have completed removing objects type '*a*' for add at the command line to start adding objects to the selection set once again. Press Return to complete the command.

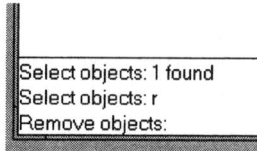

```
Select objects: 1 found
Select objects: r
Remove objects:
```

Figure 4.7   Removing objects from the selection set.

We have seen how a regular rectangular window selection set is created. Now we can look at how to create an irregularly shaped window or polygon to select the objects. In Figure 4.8(a) the *Erase* command has been used followed by '*wp*' for window polygon typed at the command line. Working anticlockwise you can then enclose

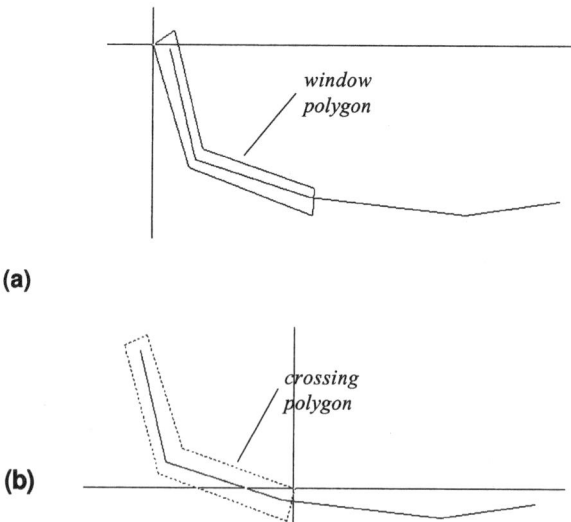

window polygon

(a)

crossing polygon

(b)

Figure 4.8   (a) Window polygon; **(b)** crossing polygon.

the objects finishing approximately at the point you started. In Figure 4.8(b) Erase has been used but followed this time with '*cp*' for crossing polygon. Starting from the right the objects can be enclosed, again ending at roughly the start point. Remember that the crossing polygon window is shown with its usual broken line boundary and it will select any objects not fully enclosed.

Using the Toolbox for Editing

The editing tools in the Toolbox are located on the bottom row as shown in Figure 4.9. When the Toolbox is located at the side of the drawing editor, the editing tools take up the bottom six rows. Remember that this arrangement could change if you customize your Toolbox. Any of the previously described methods for creating a selection set can be used.

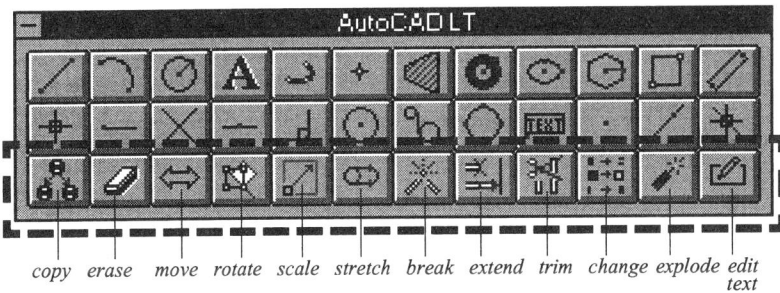

copy erase   move rotate scale stretch break extend trim change explode edit
                                                                                    text

Figure 4.9   The Toolbox with the editing tools highlighted.

Copy

This command duplicates items within the drawing. To copy you create a selection set and specify a start point and finishing point for the object copied; these points are known as the base point and second point of displacement respectively as shown in Figure 4.10.

Erase

To erase an object or objects choose the eraser icon and click the left mouse button on the object to be removed. The object will turn into a broken line effect to indicate that it has been chosen. Remember that window selections can also be made as described earlier.

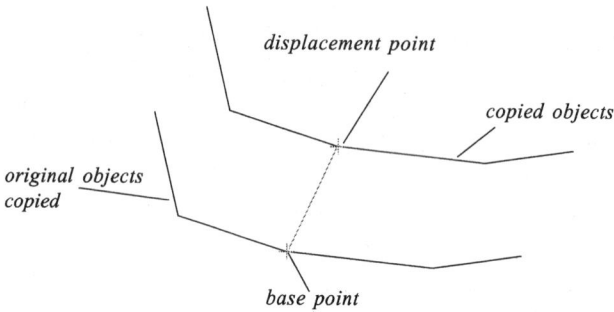

Figure 4.10 Copying objects.

As shown in Figure 4.11 you may have 'blips' or pickpoints which are small crosses on the screen where you have clicked on a selection. The screen may be refreshed with *Redraw* from the Toolbox (if it exists in your Toolbox), by pressing F7 twice (this turns the screen grid on and off quickly and refreshes the screen simultaneously) or by *View/Redraw* from the pull-down menu.

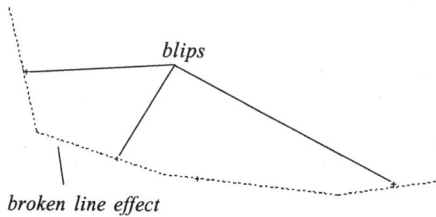

Figure 4.11 The effects of erase.

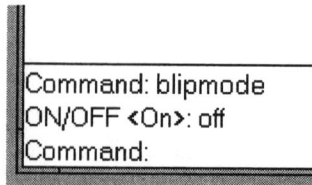

```
Command: blipmode
ON/OFF <On>: off
Command:
```

Figure 4.12 Blipmode typed at the command line.

Blips can become annoying as they fill the screen but there is an easy method of turning them off permanently: type *Blipmode* at the command line and set to '*off*' as shown in Figure 4.12 or use the S*ettings/Drawing Aids* pull-down menu and click the checkmark off in the Blips checkbox.

Move

The move command allows objects to be moved from their original position and still maintain their alignment and orientation. This command is similar to the *Copy* command as it has a base point and a point of displacement as shown in Figure 4.13.

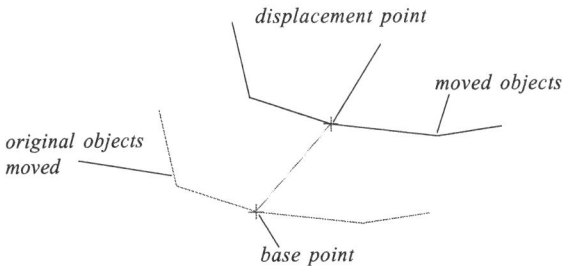

Figure 4.13   Moving objects.

Rotate

The Rotate command allows you to rotate objects about a defined base point by specifying a rotation angle or a reference angle that

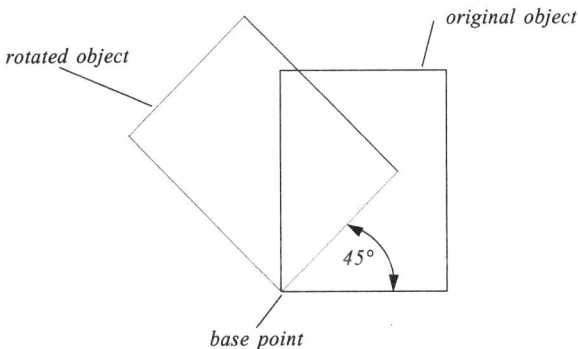

Figure 4.14   Rotating objects.

you indicate by picking points. Figure 4.14 shows objects rotated by 45° about a base point which, in this case, is the bottom left of the rectangle. AutoCAD LT uses a rubber band cursor from the base point to the new angle which you can manipulate on screen or insert a figure at the command line as we have done here.

Scale
Objects can be made smaller or larger with this command using a scale factor or a reference relative to a specified base point. If the scale factor entered on the command line is less than 1, the object is reduced in size; e.g 0.5 will reduce the object to half of its original size as shown in Figure 4.15. If the figure is greater than 1, the object will be enlarged proportionately.

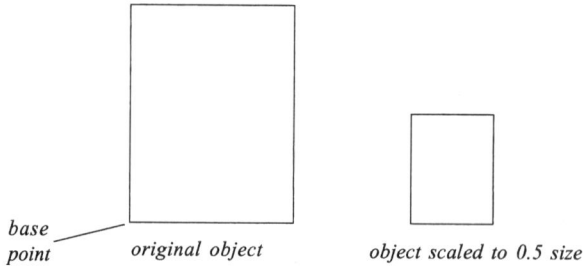

*base ___
point*   *original object*   *object scaled to 0.5 size*

Figure 4.15   Scaling by scaling factor.

If you use a reference to scale then you specify a reference point (1) and a second point (2) followed by the new length from 1 to 2. In the

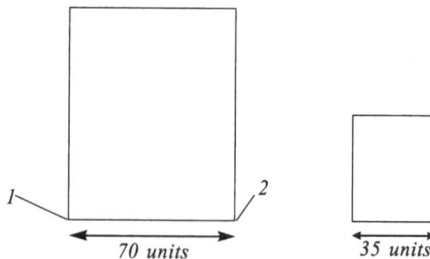

70 units   *35 units*

Figure 4.16   Scaling by reference.

example shown in Figure 4.16 the original length was 70 units and the new length of 35 units reduces the whole of the object correspondingly.

Stretch

You can stretch an object to make it longer or shorter and a base point and point of displacement are specified. The object(s) must be selected with a *crossing window* only, otherwise the stretch will not work. Stretching using relative or polar coordinates gives accuracy but is not essential. The right-hand side of the object in Figure 4.17 is being stretched where the endpoints of the top and bottom lines are moved.

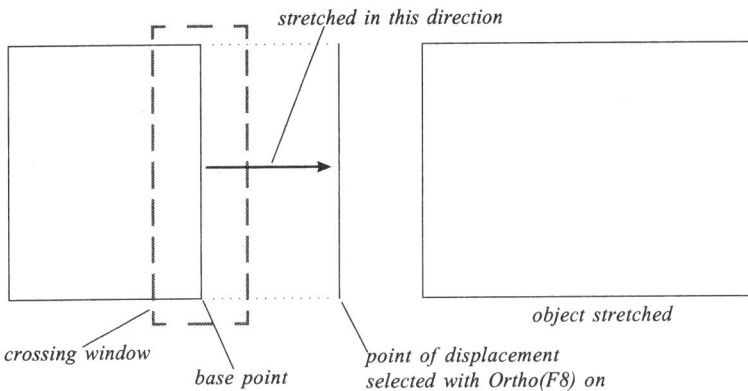

stretched in this direction

object stretched

crossing window

base point

point of displacement
selected with Ortho(F8) on

Figure 4.17 Stretching objects.

Break

The *Break* command works only on circles, arcs, lines and polylines allowing you to erase a section of a circle to become an arc, break lines into two, remove a section of a line or break and remove an end of a line. It does not use the usual noun/verb selection set method. Break asks you to select the object to break and the point that you pick on the object becomes the start point of the break. If, however, you type in '*f*' for first you are then invited to pick a first and second point as shown in Figures 4.18 and 4.19. Remember that with a circle or arc the erased portion will always be in the anticlockwise direction so it is good practice to pick your points in an anticlockwise manner.

second point

first point

original circle   broken circle

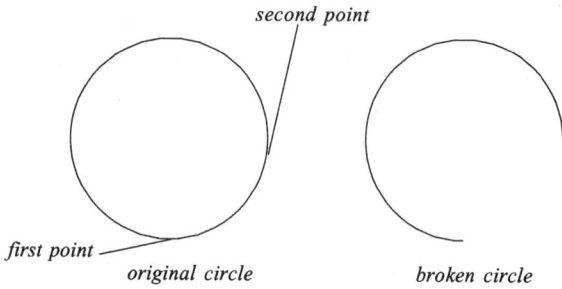

Figure 4.18   The effects of breaking a circle.

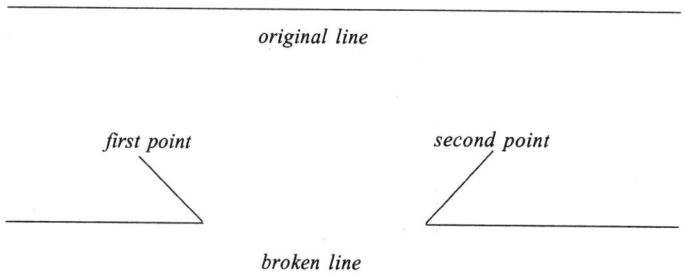

original line

first point   second point

broken line

Figure 4.19   Breaking a line.

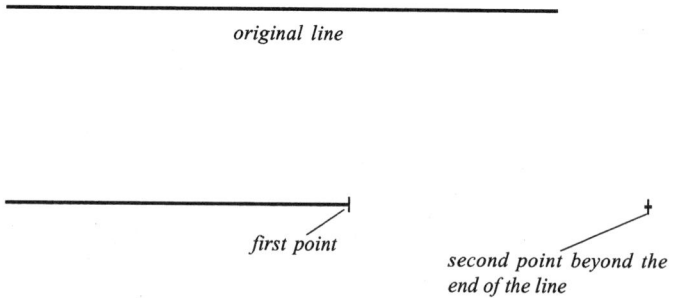

original line

first point

second point beyond the
end of the line

Figure 4.20   Breaking a line beyond its endpoint.

The second point need not be a point on the object and as shown in Figure 4.20 the line is broken from the first point to its end because the second point chosen is beyond the end of the line.

Extend

Extend does what its name implies. It extends an object to touch another by moving its endpoint. In Figure 4.21 the horizontal line is extended to touch the vertical line. You are requested to select the boundary edges by selecting both objects, the horizontal and vertical lines, and then to select the object to extend which, in the example, is the horizontal line. The horizontal line will automatically stop at the vertical line.

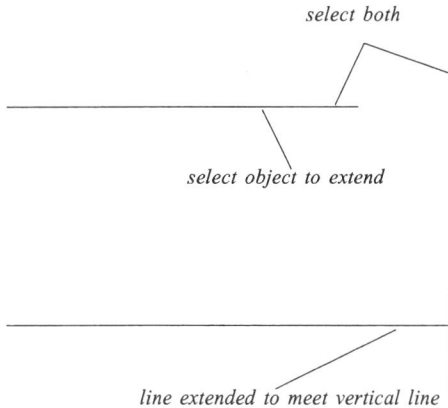

select both

select object to extend

line extended to meet vertical line

Figure 4.21   Extending one line to another.

Trim

Trim removes a part of an object especially when it projects beyond another. Figure 4.22 again shows a horizontal and vertical line with the horizontal line extending beyond the vertical. The *Trim* command asks for the cutting edge and then the object to be trimmed. You can pick either side of the cutting edge, the vertical line in our example, to trim and the line is trimmed back to the cutting edge.

In Figure 4.23 we show how two vertical lines act as the cutting edges with the result that when the horizontal line between them is chosen as the object to be trimmed, it is erased up to the two cutting edges.

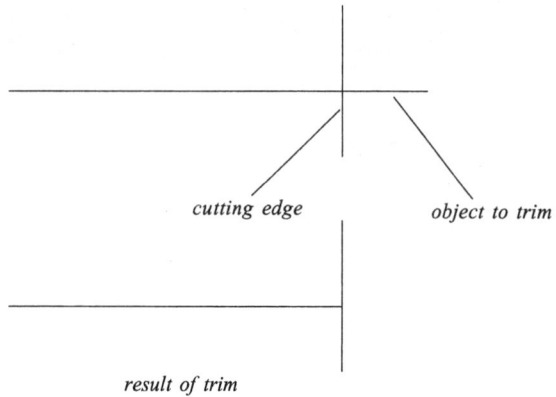

Figure 4.22   Trimming objects.

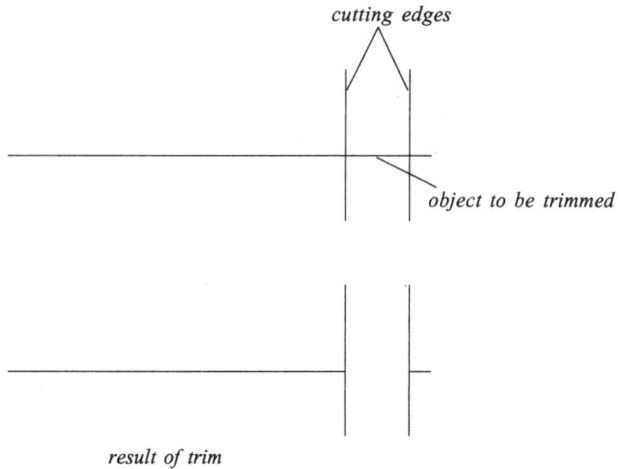

Figure 4.23   Trimming an object between two cutting edges.

Change

Change allows you to modify the properties of objects in the drawing with the Change Properties dialogue box. It allows you to alter the colour, layer, linetype or thickness of an object. After Change is selected in the Toolbox and you have selected the objects to change a dialogue box appears as shown in Figure 4.24.

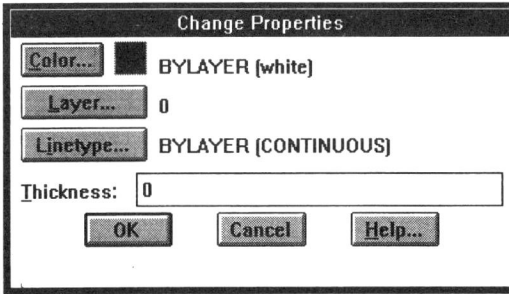

Figure 4.24 Change Properties dialogue box.

Changing a Colour Property
The Colour button activates the Select Colour dialogue box as shown in Figure 4.25. which is the same dialogue box that appears when you select the Colour button in the *Settings/Entity Creation Modes* dialogue box. You can select up to any of the 255 colours supported by AutoCAD LT.

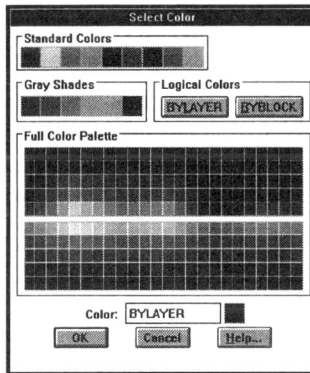

Figure 4.25 Select Colour dialogue box.

Changing a Layer Property
Setting up layers in a drawing is discussed more fully in Chapter 2 but you will probably find that at some time there will be a need to move an object from one layer to another. We do this by selecting the *Layer* button which activates the Select Layer dialogue box as shown in Figure 4.26. In our example layer 0 is shown as the default layer

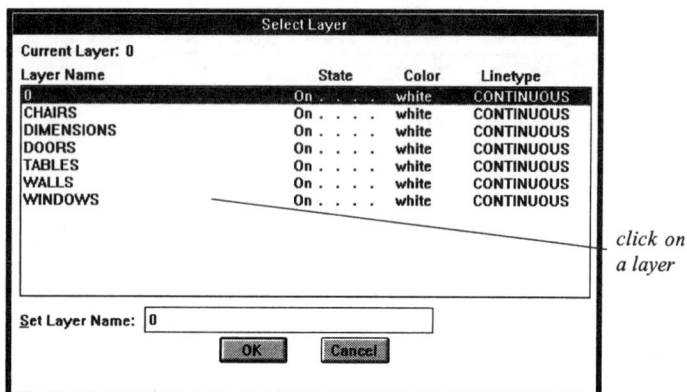

Figure 4.26 Select Layer dialogue box.

and you change to the new layer by clicking on another layer name in the list. Clicking anywhere in the row will achieve this.

Changing a Linetype Property

Changing a linetype property allows you to select any of the currently loaded linetypes. AutoCAD LT loads only the continuous linetype by default but you can change this by loading the linetypes from the files *acltiso.lin* or *aclt.lin* which we did in Chapter 2. In our example shown in Figure 4.27 we have selected the Center2 linetype to change from the continuous linetype style. When it is chosen the visual style of the line appears as shown.

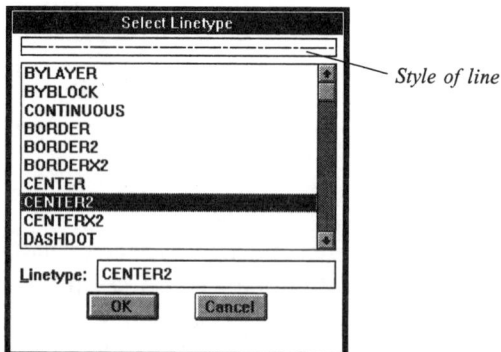

Figure 4.27 Changing the Linetype style.

After you do this you may not see an obvious change in the linetype style of the object you have chosen. This is because the *LTSCALE* (linetype scale) system variable may need to be changed.

Changing a Thickness Property

Thickness in AutoCAD LT is another name for height or extrusion distance and applies only to drawings prepared for viewing in 3D. It does not apply to 2D drawing. In Figure 4.28 we see a two-dimensional rectangle from a 2D viewpoint. Viewed from another angle the rectangle still appears in 2D. After changing the thickness we see that the rectangle is extruded upwards by the figure specified. If the rectangle is again viewed in 2D there is no obvious change to the rectangle. Drawing and viewing in 3D are discussed more fully in Chapter 3.

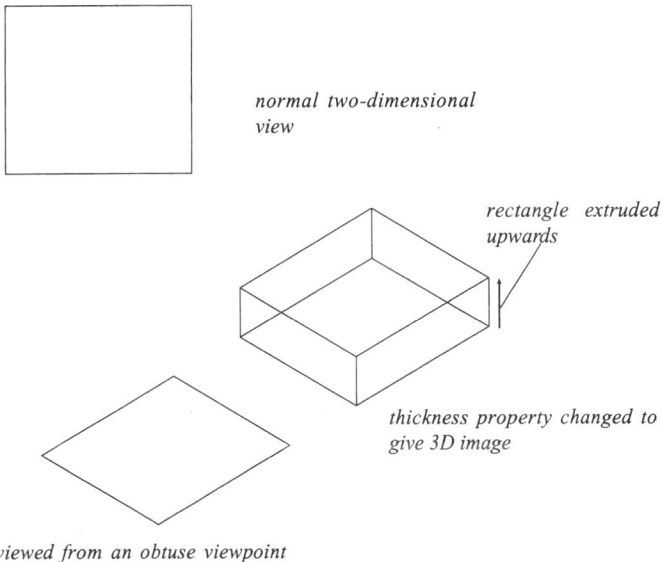

normal two-dimensional view

rectangle extruded upwards

thickness property changed to give 3D image

viewed from an obtuse viewpoint

Figure 4.28   Changing a thickness property.

Explode

Exploding an object converts it from a single object into individual entities. You can do this with polylines, rectangles, polygons, blocks and dimensions. There may not be an obvious change in the object when you use the command, particularly with polylines, rectangles and polygons which look identical. Exploding a block may convert it to its original colour. However, blocks which have been inserted with unequal X, Y and Z scales cannot be exploded. Block construction is discussed more fully in Chapter 3. Exploding a dimension will convert it to its individual objects.

Edit Text

You can change previously typed text or a block attribute definition with the Toolbox *Edit* command. You can alter typing and spelling errors or simply extend a text block. When you select the *Edit* command in the Toolbox you are invited to select the text to edit which appears in the Edit Text dialogue box as shown in Figure 4.29. Once changed in the dialogue box it is altered in the drawing when you click on OK.

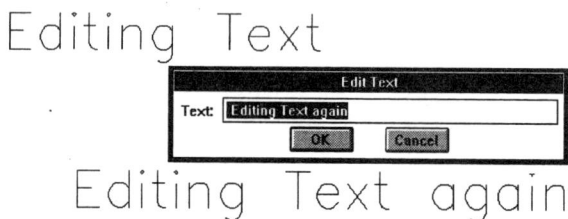

Figure 4.29　Editing text.

Array

The *Array* comand allows you to make multiple identical copies of an object in a regular circular (polar) or rectangular pattern. The Array command can be found in the Construct pull-down.

Polar Array

A polar array makes copies around a central point, rotating the objects as they are arrayed. Figure 4.30 shows a square being arrayed

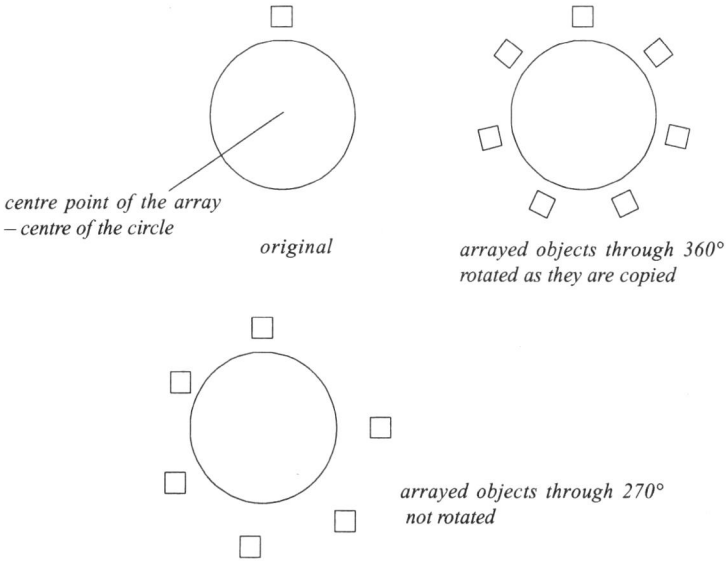

centre point of the array
– centre of the circle

original

arrayed objects through 360°
rotated as they are copied

arrayed objects through 270°
not rotated

Figure 4.30   Polar array.

around the circle. For the centre point of the array we have chosen the centre of the circle so that the arrayed object is uniformly positioned around the circle and the array covers 360°. The objects are rotated as they are copied so the copies are always an exact orientation of the original. Alternatively you can array through less than 360° and not rotate the object, as shown in the lower diagram of Figure 4.30. The number of objects can be varied but remember that the total number of arrayed objects always includes the original. The direction of the array can be controlled via *Settings/Units Control/ Direction Control* if you want to array in a clockwise direction as shown in Figure 4.31.

Rectangular Array

Rectangular arrays allow you to create copies of an original object in rows and columns in any direction by specifying the distances between the rows and columns as shown in Figure 4.32. Remember that when specifying these distances the dimensions of the original object must be included otherwise overlaps will occur where they were not intended.

108 *Editing your Drawings*

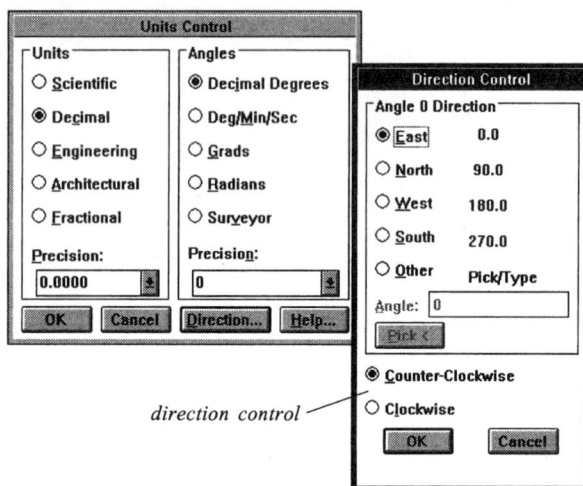

Figure 4.31 Changing the direction of the polar array.

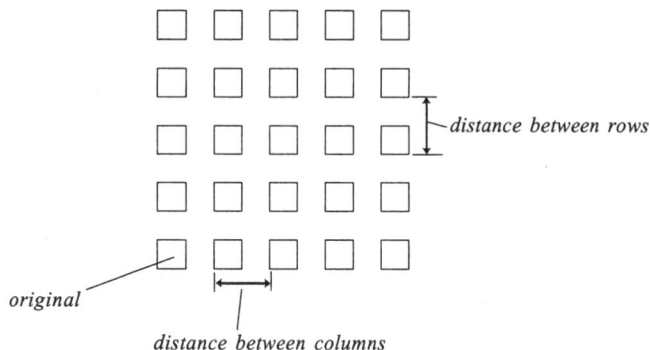

distance between rows

original

distance between columns

Figure 4.32 Rectangular array.

AutoCAD LT helps you remember which are the rows and columns
when it asks you for information by placing horizontal and vertical
lines in the command line as shown in Figure 4.33.

Figure 4.32 shows the array moving in a positive x and positive y
direction which is the default direction. However, you can change
this by placing a minus (–) sign in front of the distance between rows
and/or columns to change the direction of the array. Figure 4.34 shows

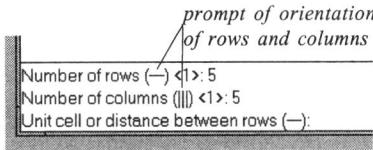

prompt of orientation
of rows and columns

```
Number of rows (—) <1>: 5
Number of columns (|||) <1>: 5
Unit cell or distance between rows (—):
```

Figure 4.33 Array orientation prompt.

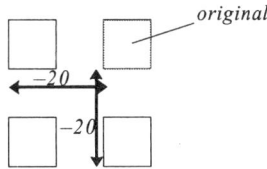

original

−20

−20

Figure 4.34 Arraying in a negative direction.

an array with two rows and two columns and a distance between the rows and columns both set at −20 units.

AutoCAD LT also allows you to create a rotated rectangular array by changing the snap rotation angle. To change this angle, which

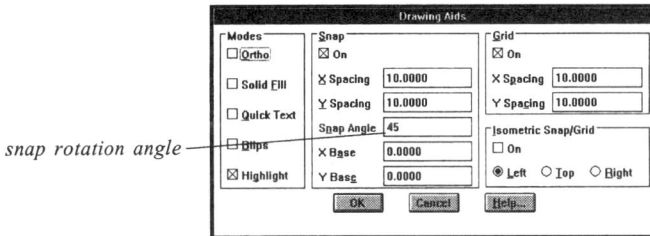

snap rotation angle

```
                          Drawing Aids
Modes            Snap                    Grid
□ Ortho          ⊠ On                    ⊠ On
□ Solid Fill     X Spacing  10.0000      X Spacing  10.0000
□ Quick Text     Y Spacing  10.0000      Y Spacing  10.0000
                 Snap Angle  45          Isometric Snap/Grid
□ Blips          X Base      0.0000      □ On
⊠ Highlight      Y Base      0.0000      ◉ Left  ○ Top  ○ Right

              [ OK ]   [ Cancel ]   [ Help... ]
```

Figure 4.35 Snap rotation angle.

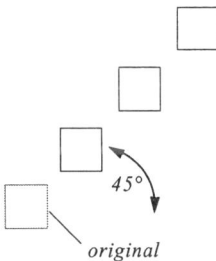

45°

original

Figure 4.36 Rotated array.

defaults to 0, use *Settings/Drawing Aids* and change the *Snap Angle* to the angle required as shown in Figure 4.35.

As shown in Figure 4.36, when you subsequently use the rectangular array command the array will align itself to the new snap angle. Remember to reset to 0° when you have completed.

Mirror

Found in the *Construct* pull-down, you are able to make reflected copies with the *Mirror* command. The copies are replicated around a central axis and you can retain the original or delete it. In Figure 4.37 an L-shaped object has been mirrored with the copy replicated as a mirror image and the original retained. You will see that the text in the mirrored image has also been mirrored in the first diagram which is not the required result. This is because the system variable *mirrtext* defaults to 1 so that all text is mirrored. Before using the mirror command type *mirrtext* at the command line, set it to 0 and the text will read the correct way.

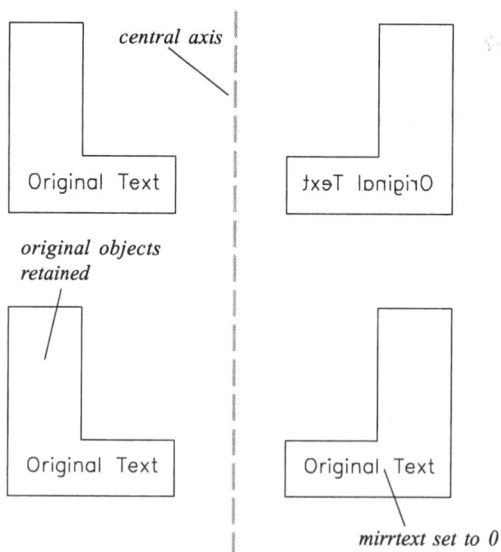

Figure 4.37   Using Mirror with the Mirrtext system variable.

In the example, ortho and snap have been set on so that the first and second mirror points (the central axis) can be picked quickly. You could of course draw a construction line.

Chamfer

The *chamfer* command places an angled or bevelled line between two intersecting lines. After activating the command you will first need to set up the chamfer distances with the distance option in the command (type '*d*' at the command line). In Figure 4.38 our example shows the first chamfer distance set at 10 and the second chamfer distance set at 20. Once you have set the chamfer distances the command finishes which can be a little alarming. Re-activate the command (press the spacebar or Return) and pick the first line to apply the first chamfer distance and the second line to apply the second distance.

Fillet

Found in the *Construct* pull-down, the *Fillet* command places an arc between lines, arcs or circles. After activating the command you will need to set up the fillet radius with '*r*'. In Figure 4.39 we have set a radius of 20. Like the *Chamfer* command, after setting up the radius, the command finishes automatically. Re-activate the command and pick the two objects to make the fillet.

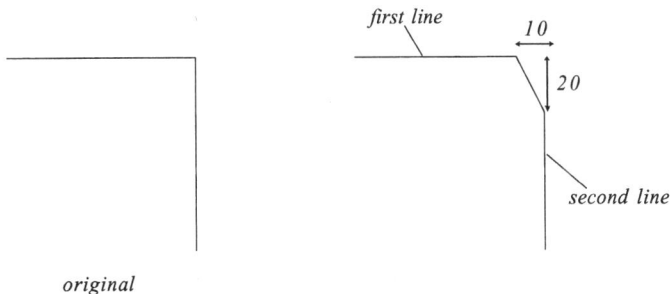

first line

10

20

second line

original

Figure 4.38   Chamfer and chamfer distances.

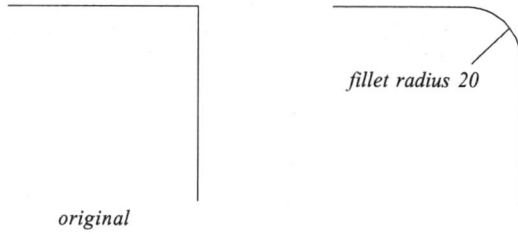

original

Figure 4.39   Fillet command.

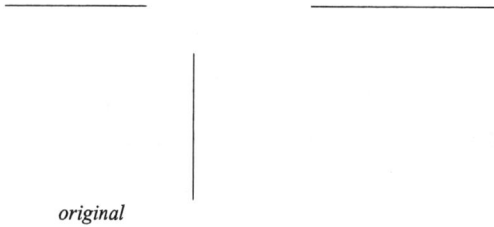

original

Figure 4.40   Fillet command with a fillet radius of 0.

This command is useful for joining two adjacent lines with a fillet radius of 0. Figure 4.40 shows the two lines before and after applying the command.

5 Plotting your Drawings

When you have completed your drawing you will be ready to repro-
duce a copy of the drawing on paper or other material (commonly
called 'hard copy') from a printer or plotter. You can, of course, print
at any time whether the drawing is complete or not and this is often
done on a lower quality material for checking purposes prior to the
final plot being done.

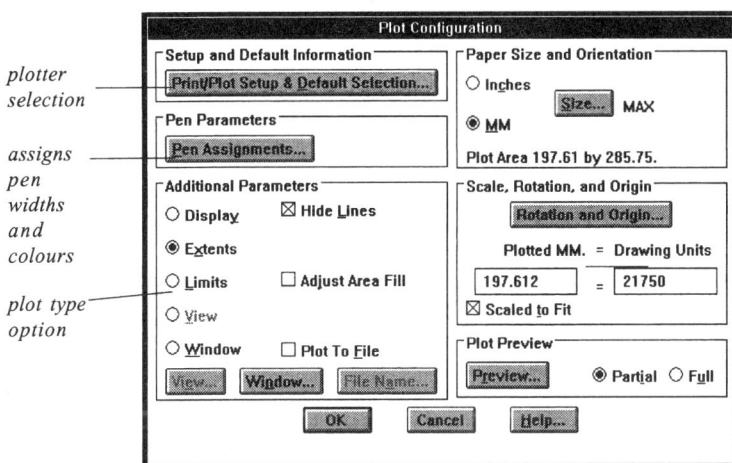

Figure 5.1   The Print/Plot dialogue box.

To Plot a Drawing

From the *File* menu select *Print/Plot* or from the Toolbar click on
the printer icon. A dialogue box appears as shown in Figure 5.1.

The Print/Plot Setup and Default Selection

This is where you select the output device. AutoCAD LT is already
configured for more than one plotter automatically, including the
system printer. To change a printer, select the *Print/Plot Setup* button as shown in Figure 5.2. This box is replaced with that shown in

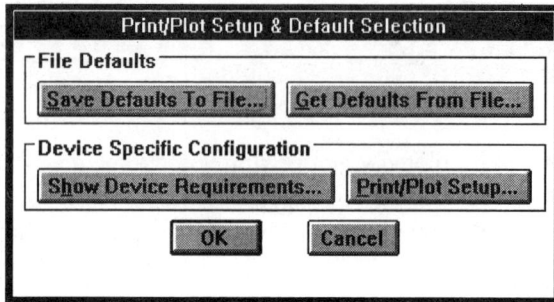

Figure 5.2   Print/Plot Setup and Default Selection.

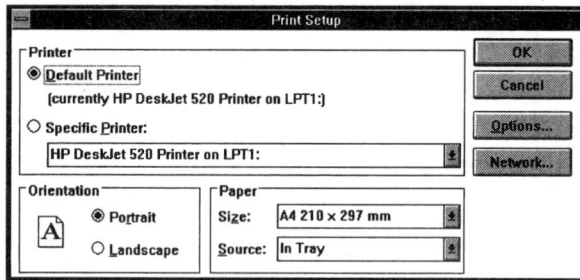

Figure 5.3   Print Setup dialogue box.

Figure 5.3 which will show the default printer along with a list of the specific printer drivers available.

Pen Parameters

This section of the plot dialogue box allows pen widths to be assigned to the colour of an object on the drawing. By assigning colours to objects in the drawing the objects can be associated with particular layers or conventions and company standards. In addition, different linetypes can be assigned to a particular colour via this box, but generally it is easier to change the linetype on the drawing itself rather than at plotting time as the printer may not support hardware linetypes. Figure 5.4 shows pen 1 chosen and ready for amendment. Remember that if you are plotting to a monchrome printer, all colours will

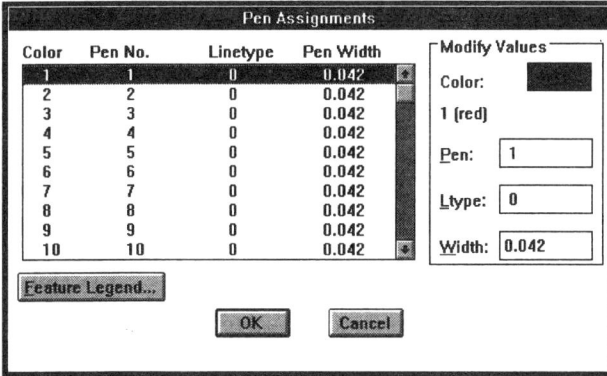

Figure 5.4 Pen Assignments dialogue box.

print as one colour (usually black). Also, if you are plotting to a printer, pen thicknesses may not be able to be changed to show different line widths on the hard copy. The same applies to polylines with widths greater than zero.

Additional Parameters

This part of the dialogue box sets either the plot area for the display already on screen at that time, the extent of the drawing, an area of the drawing which is chosen by the Window option, the limits of the drawing, or a previously saved view.

Hidden lines are specified if a 3D drawing is being printed. Figure 5.5 shows the difference between the two after printing.

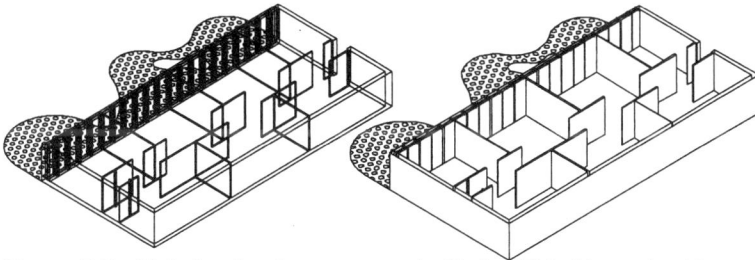

Figure 5.5 Plot showing lines removed with the Hide Lines checkbox.

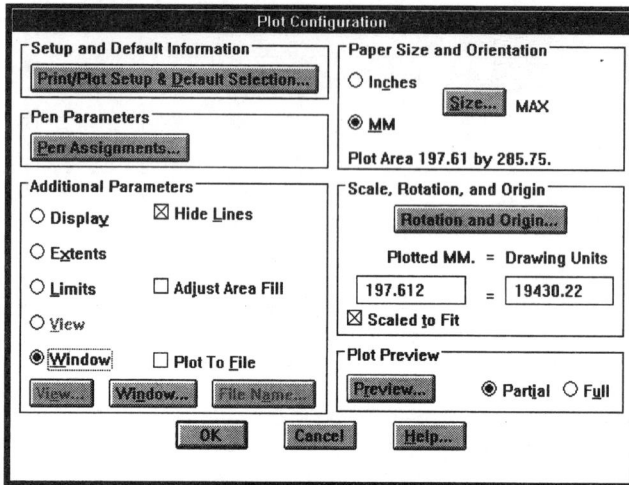

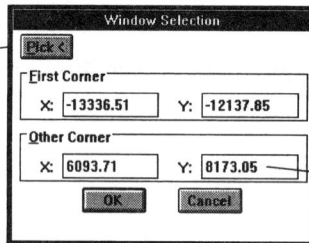

the window corners selected with this button

the window perimeter selected by coordinates

Figure 5.6 The Print/Plot dialogue box with the Window plot option selected.

Plotting a window allows you either to pick the two diagonally opposite corners of the window or alternatively to specify the x,y coordinates. Figure 5.6 shows the dialogue box if you have chosen the *Window* option. Once you have chosen your window size, it is OK'd and the Print/Plot dialogue box is reinstated.

A view is printed by selecting the view button but remember that this option is not available if no views have been saved in the drawing; this will be shown by the 'greyed out' image of the non-available button. If a view has been saved and this function is chosen a dialogue box appears for you to select the view to be printed, as shown in Figure 5.7. Once it is OK'd control returns to the Print/Plot dialogue box.

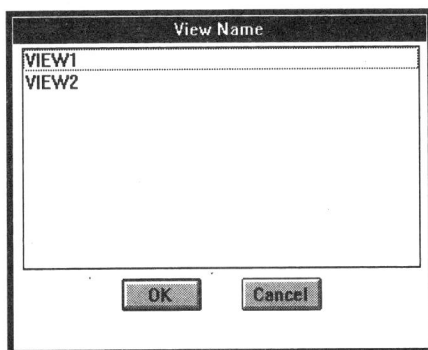

Figure 5.7 The View dialogue box showing two saved views available for plotting

If *Display*, *Extents* or *Limits* are used the resulting plots will differ greatly depending on what rotation and origin are used. For the next section we will show how this combination changes merely by changing the rotation angle from 0° to 90°.

To change the angle the Rotation and Origin button is selected and a dialogue box appears as in Figure 5.8 which shows the rotation of the drawing on the paper as 0°.

Used with the Plot Preview button it will show the result before plotting is commenced. There are two options within the plot preview – a partial and a full preview. The partial preview shows only how much of the paper will be used and is mainly used to check the

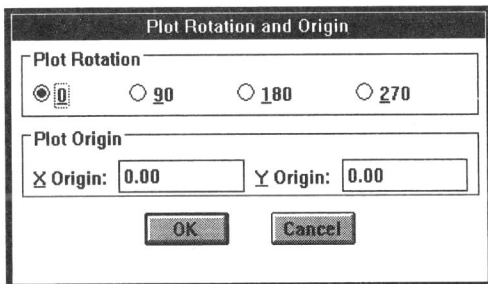

Figure 5.8 The Plot Rotation and Origin dialogue box.

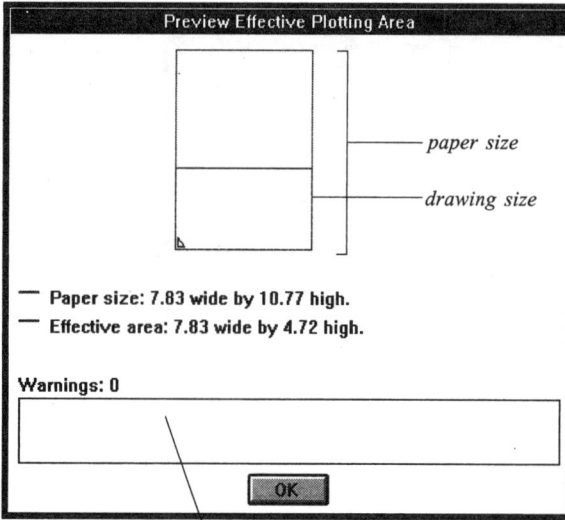

Paper size: 7.83 wide by 10.77 high.
Effective area: 7.83 wide by 4.72 high.

Warnings: 0

gives a message showing if plotted
drawing is outside the plotting area

Figure 5.9   Plot preview dialogue box using a partial preview with
0° rotation.

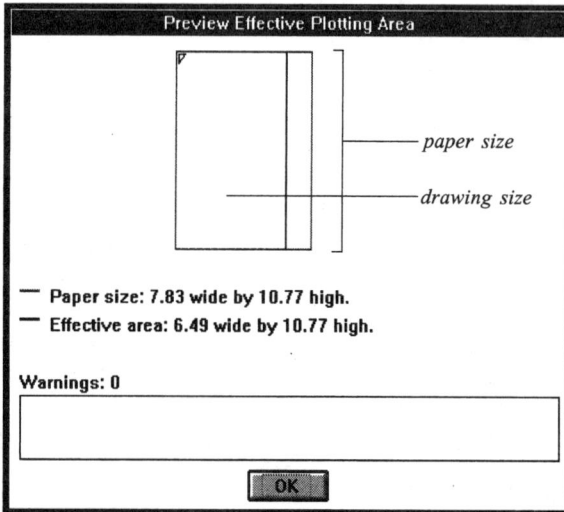

Paper size: 7.83 wide by 10.77 high.
Effective area: 6.49 wide by 10.77 high.

Warnings: 0

Figure 5.10   Plot preview using a partial preview with 90° rotation.

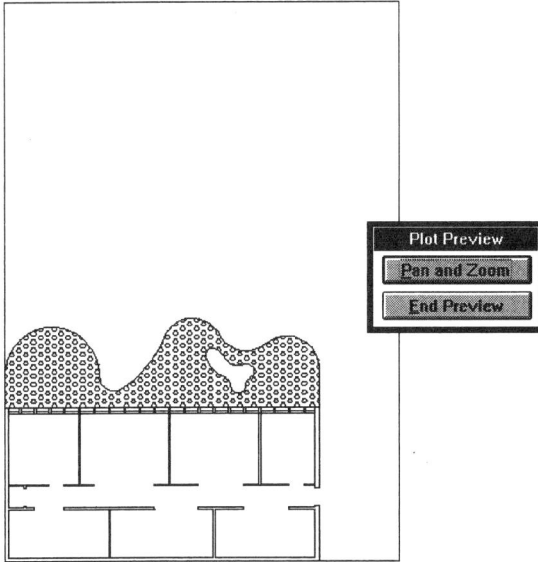

Figure 5.11   0° rotation and display plot.

position of the drawing on the paper. Figure 5.9 shows the plot with a 0° rotation, scaled to fit the paper size and to plot the display. Compare this with the situation when the plot rotation is changed to 90° as shown in Figure 5.10 where the drawing fills more of the paper.

Figure 5.11 shows a full preview of the current display, scaled to fit the current paper size and 0° rotation.

Compare again how the final output changes when the rotation angle is changed to 90° in Figure 5.12.

Figure 5.13 shows a plot to the Extents of the drawing, scaled to fit the paper size and 0° rotation. Extents plots all of the objects in the drawing. Note how the drawing fills the width of the paper, compared to Figure 5.14 where the rotation angle is 90°, and fills the length of the paper.

Figure 5.15 shows a plot preview of the limits of the drawing, scaled to fit and rotated at 0°. You will notice that the drawing seems to

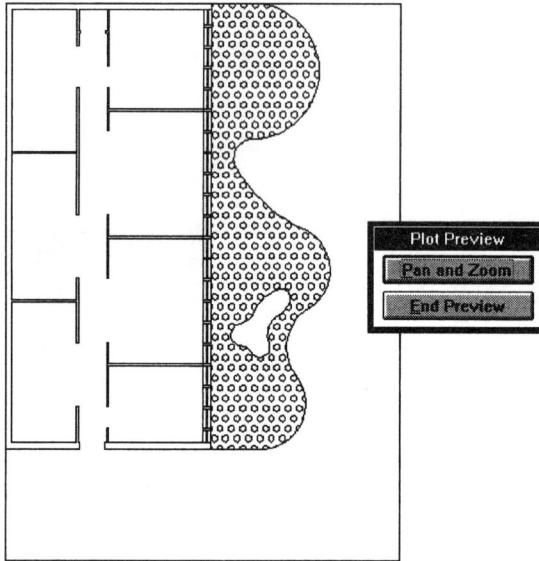

Figure 5.12   90° rotation and display plot.

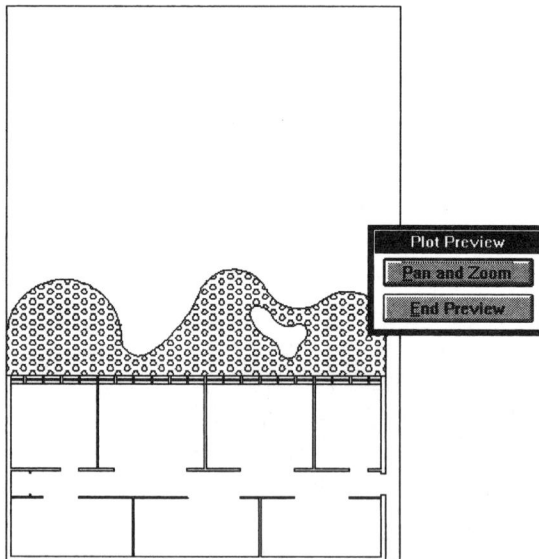

Figure 5.13   0° rotation extents plot.

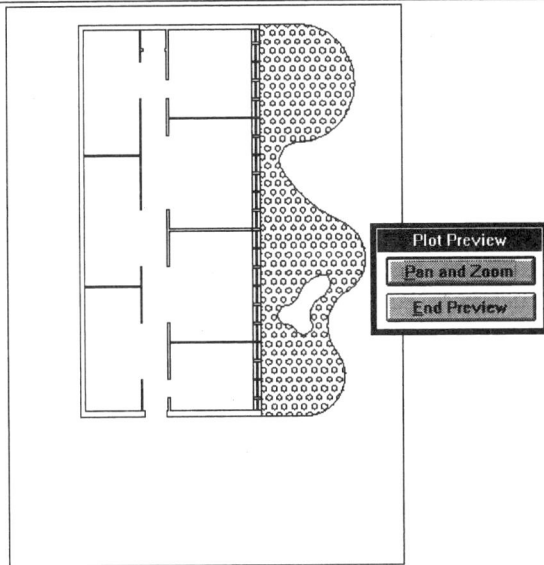

Figure 5.14   90° rotation limits plot.

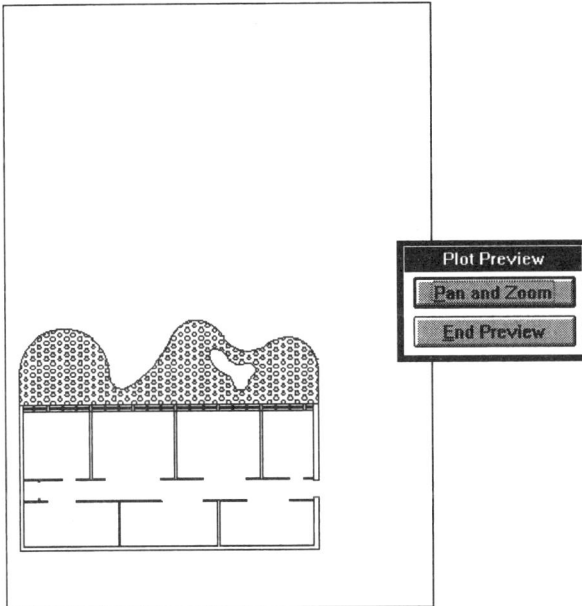

Figure 5.15   0° rotation limits plot.

have been moved but the limits of the drawing have been taken into account, so having large limits on a small drawing will affect the output.

Altering the Paper Size

You will need to plot onto different paper sizes depending on the scale of the required hard copy. An A4 system printer for example will generally only allow up to an A4 sheet size but plotters up to, say, A0 will allow sheet sizes up to the maximum. This can include the standard A sizes (A4, A3, A2, A1, A0), the B sizes and also any custom sheet sizes set by the user. The purpose of specifying the sheet size allows AutoCAD LT to show an accurate Plot Preview before plotting commences.

Altering the Drawing Position on the Paper

In AutoCAD LT the default origin position on the drawing is 0 in the x coordinate and 0 in the y coordinate, which translates to the bottom left-hand corner of the plotted drawing.

This origin position can be changed, particularly if your plotter has automatic margins set. Printers also have a margin but not usually as wide as a plotter. If you find that the left and bottom edges of your plotted drawing are cropped, it is worth altering the plot origin settings through the *Rotation and Origin* button in the Plot Configuration dialogue box. Figure 5.16 shows the plot origin changed to 20,20 (x,y) and the resulting movement of the drawing on the final plot.

This feature can be used to good effect by plotting twice on the same sheet of paper. By re-installing in the printer the sheet of paper that has the first plot as shown in Figure 5.16 and changing the plot origin you can plot a second drawing on the same sheet (Figure 5.17). In Figure 5.17 a window plot has been selected for the second plot and the x,y plot origin changed to 150,50.

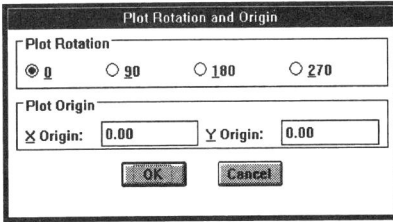

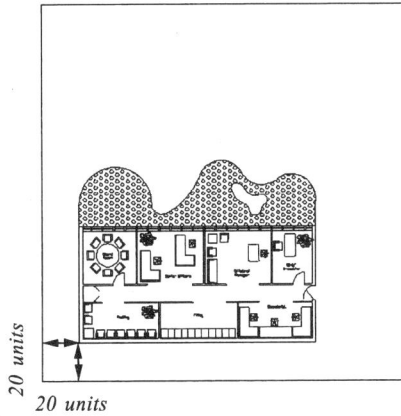

Figure 5.16　Change of plot origin.

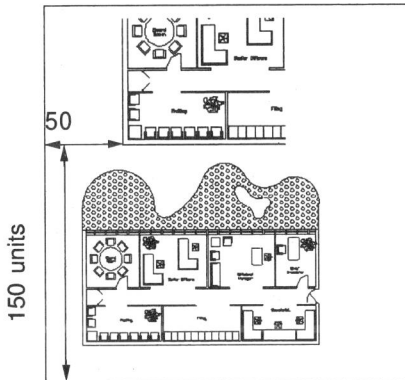

Figure 5.17　Second plot showing the result of moving the plot origin and
plotting on original sheet.

The Scale of the Plotted Drawing

Initially, this is one of the most confusing parts of CAD drafting. Whereas with manual drafting the drawing is immediately produced to a scale, CAD insists that we draw to full size and scale the drawing only at plot time. The concept of viewing a drawing on screen which, full size, is a few kilometres long can be very confusing. However, if you follow a few simple rules it will become as easy as manual drafting:

- Always consider the final scale before starting to draw, e.g. 1:500 or 1:50.
- How large should the final plot be?
- What height should text be to be readable at the chosen scale?
- If Mview viewports have been used in paper space, what should be the zoom factors in each of the viewports?
- What scale should the linetypes be?
- What dimension scale (DIMSCALE) value should be used?

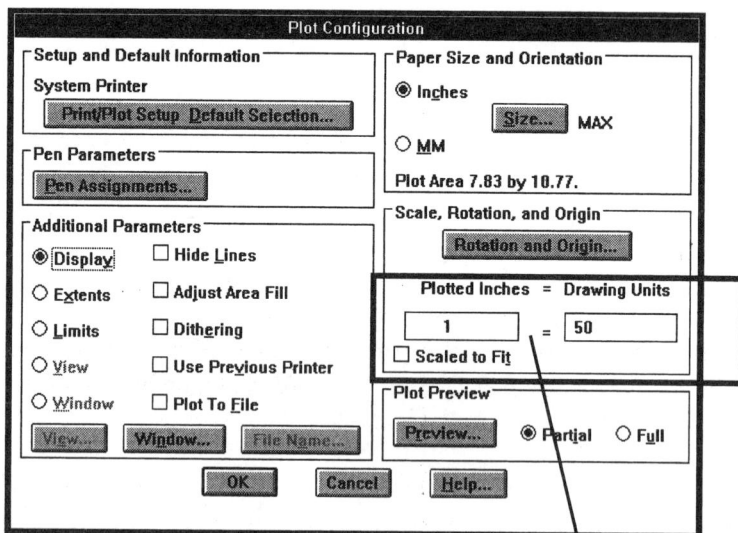

type scale in here

Figure 5.18 Print/Plot dialogue box showing scale 1:50.

Let's suppose that you want your drawing to be at a final plotted scale of 1:50 (Figure 5.18).

AutoCAD LT will physically scale down your drawing 50 times smaller than it was produced. The plot factor becomes 50. If you require text to be 5 mm high on the final plot, set a text height of 250 mm (250/50 = 5).

Also, you can set a DIMSCALE of 50 and a linetype scale of 50 as well.

Model Space and Paper Space Plotting

You will do most of your drawing in Model Space; Paper Space should be reserved for title blocks and border detail (the difference between Model and Paper Space and their manipulation is discussed in Chapter 3). The golden rule is that if you are plotting from Model Space, you plot to a scale, e.g. 1:50. If Paper Space plotting is used, a scale of 1:1 is set.

Paper Space allows the whole drawing sheet to be composed in a Paper Space viewport with any annotations. Paper Space is ideal for entering text at its full height, for example 5 mm high text can be entered at 5 mm height which is not the case in Model Space where, as we have seen, a scaling factor has to be applied depending upon the eventual plotted scale of the drawing.

Saving a Plot Configuration

When you want to plot a drawing you create a plot scale, paper size, pen assignments, view to plot, rotation of the drawing, etc. AutoCAD LT allows you to save these particular plot configuration settings in the *Print/Plot Setup & Default Selection* dialogue box as shown in Figure 5.19.

Figure 5.20 shows the dialogue box after pressing the button in Figure 5.19. You can give the file any name you wish. The file extension .PCP is automatically added by AutoCAD LT.

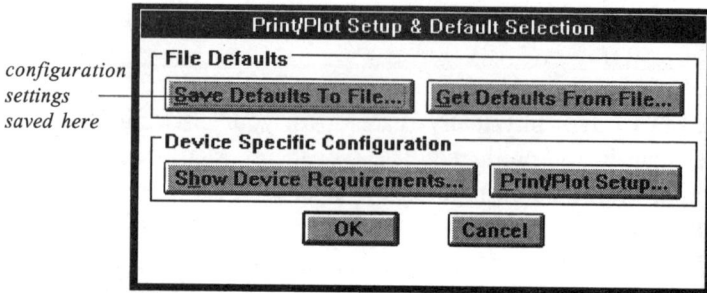

Figure 5.19   Print/Plot Setup dialogue box.

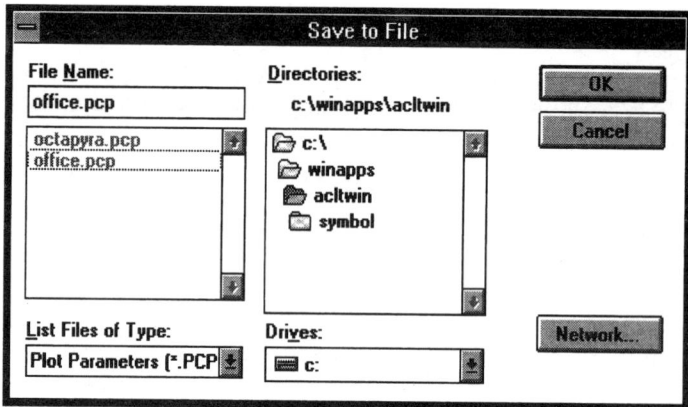

Figure 5.20   Saving plot configuration settings.

It is possible and desirable to save these configurations for any
changes in plotting circumstances you may have; this will save time
later on. To recall any saved changes you simply press the *Get Defaults from File* button.

Plotting to a File

Instead of plotting directly to a printer AutoCAD LT allows you to
save the drawing in a file. You may need to do this to enable plot
spooling software to print to a shared network device or to create a
plot file for importing the drawing into programs that read only plot
file formats.

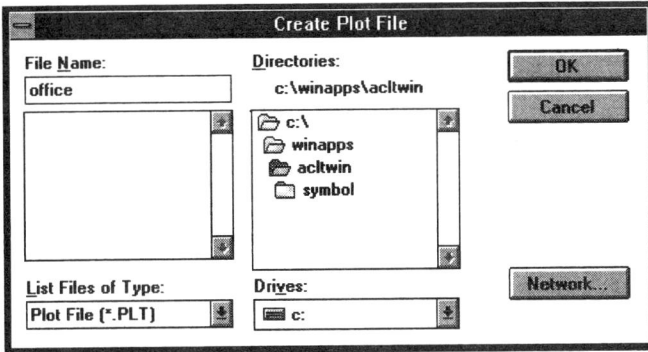

Figure 5.21 The Create Plot File dialogue box.

Figure 5.21 shows the Plot configuration dialogue box after the *Plot to File* box is checked and then overlaid by the Create Plot File dialogue box. Where 'unnamed' is shown, you would enter a meaningful plot file name such as 'office'.

A Final Note on Plotting

If you create a monochrome plot (black and white) on a PostScript device you may need to change all of your layer colours to black as the printer could use dot halftones to represent the colours. The resulting plot could show solid lines for the black objects in your drawing but dotted lines for any objects that are coloured on screen. A preferable alternative to changing the layer colours is to use the *Setup/ Options/Advanced/All Colours* to black in the Windows Printers dialogue box.

6 General Information

Hardware and Software

To be able to run AutoCAD LT you will need the following hardware:

- A PC (Personal Computer) with an 80386, 80486 or Pentium CPU with 16 Mb RAM.
- A hard disk with at least 20 Mb of available free space so that AutoCADLT can be loaded
- A display monitor with a VGA resolution or higher quality
- A pointing device, i.e. a mouse preferably with three buttons.

To print your drawings you will also need a printer or plotter.
The software required is:

- MS-DOS version 3.3 or higher
- Windows 3.1 or higher
- AutoCAD LT.

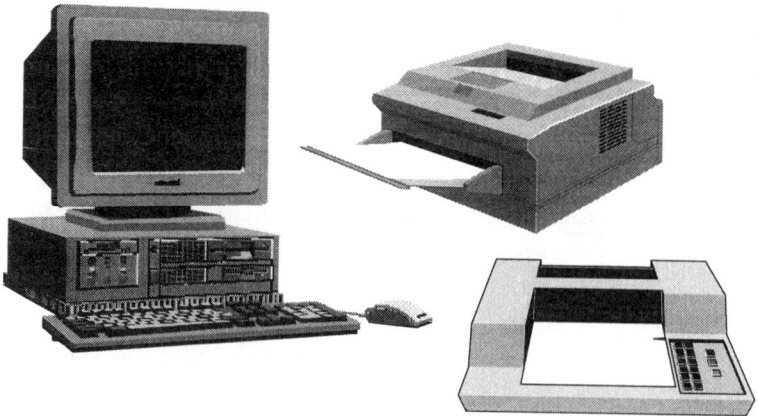

Figure 6.1 A typical computer, printer, plotter.

Command and Feature Overview

Below is a list of the AutoCAD LT commands and how to activate them. They are shown by

❑ Command name

❑ How to access the command through the icons

❑ How to access the command through the menu

❑ The keyboard shortcut (known as an alias)

❑ The description of the command

Command	*Icon*	*Menu*	*Keyboard*	*Description*
3DPOLY				Creates 3D polylines
ABOUT			AB	Displays information about the AutOCAD LT loaded
APERTURE			AP	Changes the size of the object snap target box
ARC		Draw/Arc	A	Draws an arc subject to different options
AREA		Assist/ Area	AA	Calculates the area and perimeter of selected objects
ARRAY		Construct/ Array	AR	Copies objects in a circular or rectangular pattern
ATTDEF			AD	Creates an attribute definition attached to a block

Command	Icon	Menu	Keyboard	Description
ATTDISP			AT	Controls attribute visibility
ATTEDIT			AE	Edits attribute values
ATTEXT			AX	Extracts attribute data from the drawing into a predefined file
BASE		Settings/ Drawing/ Base	BA	Controls the insertion base point of the current drawing
BHATCH		Draw/ Boundary Hatch		Fills a closed area with a hatch pattern
BLIPMODE			BM	Controls the display of 'pickpoints' on screen
BLOCK			B	Creates a reusable symbol
BMAKE		Construct/ Make Block		Creates a reusable symbol through a dialogue box
BOUNDARY		Draw/ Boundary		Draws a closed polyline boundary
BREAK		Modify/ Break	BR	Splits an object into two or erases part of an object
CHAMFER		Construct/ Chamfer	CF	Creates a bevelled edge on objects

Command	Icon	Menu	Keyboard	Description
CHANGE			CH	Changes the properties of objects
CHPROP			CR	Changes the layer, linetype, colour, linetype scale factor and thickness (height) of an object
CIRCLE		Draw/ Circle	C	Draws a circle
COLOR			CO	Globally sets the colour of new objects (ignores any layer colours already set)
COPY		Modify/	CO	Duplicates objects either singly or in multiples
COPYCLIP		Edit/ Copy Vectors	CC	Copies selected objects to the Windows clipboard
COPYEMBED		Edit/ Copy Embed	CE	Copies selected objects to embed in another program
COPYIMAGE		Edit/ Copy Image	CI	Copies a selected portion of the current drawing in bitmap format
COPYLINK		Edit/ Copy Link	CL	Copies the current screen view to the Windows clipboard for linking to OLE applications

Command	Icon	Menu	Keyboard	Description
DDATTDEF		File/ Import/ Export Attributes Out	DAX	Creates an attribute
DDATTE		Modify/ Edit Attribute	DE	Edits attribute values
DDATTEXT		File/ Import/ Export/	DAX	Extracts attribute data from the drawing into a pre-defined file
DDCHPROP		Modify/ Change	DC	Changes the layer, linetype, colour, linetype scale factor, properties and thickness (height) of an object
DDEDIT		Modify/ Edit Text	ED,TE	Edits attributes and text
'DDEMODES		Settings/ Entity Modes	EM	Sets properties for new objects
'DDGRIPS		Settings/ Grip Style	GR	Turns grips on and assigns colour
DDIM		Draw/ Insert Block	DM	Creates dimension styles

Command	Icon	Menu	Keyboard	Description
DDINSERT		Draw/ Insert Block	I	Inserts a block or another drawing into the current drawing
'DDLMODES		Settings/ Layer Control	LD	Opens the Layer Control dialogue box
DDMODIFY		Modify/ Modify Entity		Controls the properties of objects
'DDOSNAP		Assist/ Object Snap	OS	Opens the Object Snap dialogue box
'DDTYPE		Settings/ Point Style		Opens the Point Style dialogue box
DDRENAME		Modify/ Rename	DR	Changes the name of objects
'DDRMODES		Settings/ Drawing Aids	DA	Opens the Drawing Aids dialogue box
'DDSELECT		Settings/ Selection Style	SL	Sets selection modes of objects
DDUCS		Assist/ Named UCS	UC	Manages defined UCSs

Command	Icon	Menu	Keyboard	Description
DDUCSP		Assist/ Preset UCS		Chooses a preset UCS
'DDUNITS		Settings/ Unit Style	DU	Opens the Units Style dialogue box for angle, units type and precision display
DELAY				Used in scripts to time a pause of a slide
DIM			D	Activates dimensioning mode
DIM1			D1	Opens the Dimensioning Mode dialogue box
'DIST		Assist/ Distance	DI	Measures distance and angle between two points
DIVIDE		Construct/ Divide		Places evenly spaced points around the perimeter of an object
DLINE		Draw/ Double Line	DL	Draws a double line
DONUT		Draw/ Donut	DO	Draws a filled concentric circle
DSVIEWER		Settings/ Aerial View	DS	Opens the Aerial View window

Command	Icon	Menu	Keyboard	Description
DTEXT	A	Draw/ Text	T	Displays text on screen as it is entered – next letter position shown by a box
DVIEW		View/3D Dynamic View	DV	Displays parallel or perspective projection
DXFIN		File/ Import/ Export DXF In	DN	Imports a drawing interchange file
DXFOUT		File/ Import/ Export DXF Out	DX	Exports a drawing interchange file
ELEV			EV	Sets the elevation and thickness of new objects
ELLIPSE		Draw/ Ellipse	EL	Draws an ellipse or elliptical arc
END				Saves the drawing and exits AutoCAD LT
ERASE		Modify/ Erase	E	Deletes selected objects
EXIT				Exits AutoCAD LT
EXPLODE		Modify/ Explode	EP,X	Changes compound objects to individual objects

Command	Icon	Menu	Keyboard	Description
EXTEND		Modify/ Extend	EX	Extends an object to another
FILEOPEN				Opens a file
'FILL			FL	Controls the filling of solids and wide polylines
FILLET		Construct/ Fillet	F	Rounds the corners of selected objects
GETENV				Displays variables from the alct.ini file
'GRAPHSCR				Flips from text window to graphics window
'GRID			G	Turns on the screen grid
HANDLES				Gives a unique number to each object in the current drawing
HATCH			H	Fills a selected area with a pattern
HATCHEDIT		Modify/ Edit Hatch		Modifies an associative hatch block
'HELP		Help/ Contents		Displays online help

Command	Icon	Menu	Keyboard	Description
HIDE		View/ Hide	HI	Displays a 3D model with hidden lines removed to make it look solid
'ID		Assist/ ID Point		Returns the X, Y and Z coordinates of a point
INSERT			IN	Places a block or drawing into the current drawing
'ISOPLANE			IS	Specifies the current isometric plane
'LAYER			LA	Activates the Layer function at the command line
'LIMITS		Settings/ Drawing Limits	LM	Activates the Limits function at the command line
LINE		Draw/ Line	L	Draws a line
'LINETYPE		Settings/ Linetype Style	LT	Activates the Linetype command to load, set and create
LIST		Assist/ List	LS	Displays full database information on selected objects
'LTSCALE		Settings/ Linetype Style/ Linetype Scale	LC	Sets the scale globally of the linetypes in the current drawing

Command	Icon	Menu	Keyboard	Description
MEASURE		Construct/ Measure		Places points at intervals on an object
MIRROR		Construct/ Mirror	MI	Creates a mirrored copy of selected objects
MOVE	⇔	Modify/ Move	M	Moves an object from its current location to another at a given direction and distance
MSLIDE		File/ Import/ Export/ Mslide	ML	Creates a 'snapshot' of the current screen view
MSPACE	P		MS	Switches from Model Space to Paper Space
MULTIPLE			MU	Repeats the next command until it is cancelled
MVIEW		View/ Viewports	MV	Creates viewports in Paper Space
NEW	◻	File/ New	N	Creates a new drawing file and opens the New Drawing dialogue box
OFFSET		Construct/ Offset	OF	Copies objects in a specified distance and direction
OOPS		Modify/ Oops	OO	Reinstates erased objects

Command	Icon	Menu	Keyboard	Description
OPEN		File/ Open	OP	Opens an existing drawing file
'ORTHO			OR	Constrains cursor movement
OSNAP		Assist/ Object Snap	O	Activates Object Snap modes at the command line
'PAN		View/Pan	P	Moves the current display
PASTECLIP		Edit/Paste	PC	Inserts data from Windows clipboard
PEDIT		Modify/ Edit Polyline	PE	Edits polylines
PLAN		View/ 3D Plan View	PV	Displays the plan view of a UCS
PLINE		Draw/ Polyline	PL	Creates a 2D polyline
PLOT		File/Print Plot	PP	Opens up Print/Plot dialogue box to enable plotting of the current drawing
POINT		Draw/ Point	PT	Places a point on the drawing

Command	Icon	Menu	Keyboard	Description
POLYGON		Draw/ Polygon	PG	Draws an equilateral polyline
PREFERENCES		File/ Preferences	PF	Customizes AutoCAD LT settings
PSOUT		File/ Import/ Export/ PostScript Out	PS	Creates an Encapsulated PostScript file
PSPACE			PS	Changes from Model Space to Paper Space
PURGE		Modify/ Purge	PR	Removes unused name references from the current drawing
QSAVE		File/ Save		Saves the current drawing
QTEXT			QT	Temporarily displays text as lines to enhance speed
QUIT		File/ Exit	ET	Exits the drawing without saving it
RECTANG		Draw/ Rectangle	RC	Draws a polyline in a rectangular shape
REDO		Edit/Redo	RE	Reverses the previous UNDO command

Command	Icon	Menu	Keyboard	Description
'REDRAW		View/ Redraw	R	Refreshes the screen and deletes 'blips'
REGEN		View/ Regen	RG	Regenerates the drawing and refreshes all viewports
RENAME			RN	Changes the name of an object
RESUME				Continues an interrupted script file
REVDATE		Modify/ Date and Time		Inserts a revision time, date file and user name into the current drawing
ROTATE		Modify/ Rotate	RO	Revolves objects around a selected base point
RSCRIPT				Runs a script file
SAVE			SA	Saves the current drawing
SAVEAS		File/ Save as		Saves the current drawing with a new file name or saves an unnamed drawing
SCALE		Modify/ Scale	SC	Enlarges or reduces objects by ratio
SCRIPT		File/ Run Script	SR	Activates the Select Script File dialogue box

Command	Icon	Menu	Keyboard	Description
SELECT		Assist/ Select	SE	Places selected objects in the previous slection set
SETENV				Sets the variables in the aclt.ini file
'SETVAR				Lists and/or changes the values of system variables
SHADE		View/ Shade	SH	Displays a shaded image of the current viewport
'SNAP	S		SN	Enables cursor movement at specified intervals
SOLID		Draw/ Solid	SO	Creates a solid filled object
STRETCH		Modify/ Stretch	S	Stretches an object
STYLE			ST	Creates a named text style
TEXT			TX	Allows a single line of text to be input
TEXTSCR		Edit/ Text Window		Flips from graphics window to text window
'TIME		Assist/ Time	TI	Displays time/date detail of a drawing
TOOLBOX		Settings/ Toolbox Style		Controls the position and display of the Toolbox

Command	Icon	Menu	Keyboard	Description
TRIM		Modify/ Trim	TR	Trims objects by a defined cutting edge
U		Edit/ Undo		Reverses the most recent action
UCS		Assist/ Set UCS		Sets a User Coordinate System
UCSICON		Assist/ UCs Icon	UI	Controls the visibility of the UCS icon on the screen
UNDO			UN	Reverses a command
'UNITS			UT	Opens the Units command in the text screen
UNLOCK		File/ Unlock Files	UL	Unlocks locked files
'VIEW		View/ View	V	Saves and restores named views
VPLAYER		View/ Viewport Layer Visibility	VL	Allows the visibility of layers in viewports
VPOINT		View/ 3D Viewpoint	VP	Sets the viewing direction in a 3D model
VPORTS		View/ Viewports	VW	Allows multiple viewports on the same screen view

Command	Icon	Menu	Keyboard	Description
VSLIDE		File/ Import/ Export/ View Slide	VS	Displays a previously saved slide
WBLOCK		File/ Import/ Export/ Block Out	W	Writes a copy of a block to make it a drawing in its own right. Can then be used in other drawings
WMFIN		File/ Import/ Export/ WMF In	WI	Imports a Windows Metafile into the drawing
WMFOPTS		File/ Import/ Export/ WMF In Options		Sets the parameters for WMFIN
WMFOUT		File/ Import/ Export/ WMF Out	WO	Exports objects to a Windows Metafile
XBIND		Draw/ External Reference/ Bind Symbols	XB	Binds external references to a drawing

Command	Icon	Menu	Keyboard	Description
XREF		Draw/ External Reference	XR	Controls external references to a drawing file
'ZOOM		View/ Zoom	Z	Makes the current view larger or smaller in the current viewport

A list of hatch patterns follows on p. 146.

Hatch Patterns

AutoCAD LT comes with 53 choices of hatch pattern which are shown below.

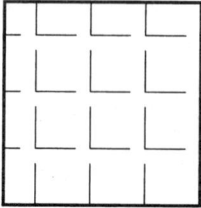

ANGLE

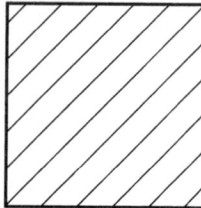

ANSI31

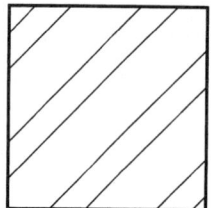

ANSI32

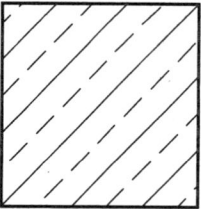

ANSI33

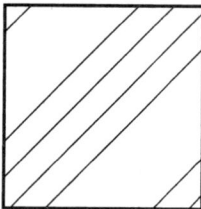

ANSI34

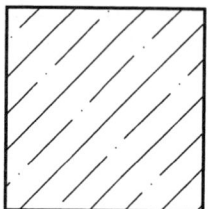

ANSI35

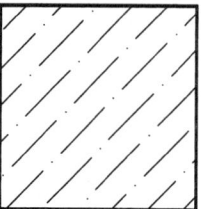

ANSI36

ANSI37

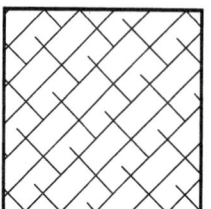

ANSI38

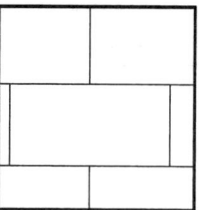

AR-B816

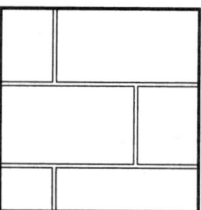

AR-B816C

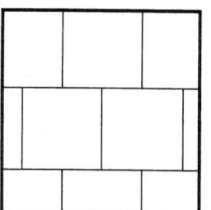

ARB-88

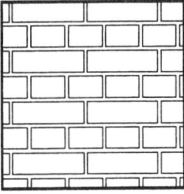

AR-BRELM

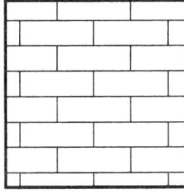

AR-BRSTD

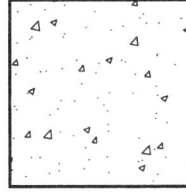

AR-CONC

AR-HBONE

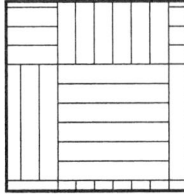

AR-PARQT

AR-BRELM

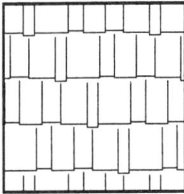

AR-RSHKE

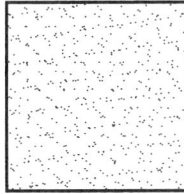

AR-SAND

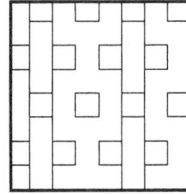

BOX

BRASS

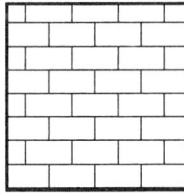

BRICK

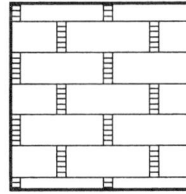

BRSTONE

CLAY

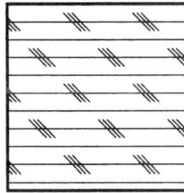

CORK

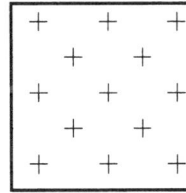

CROSS

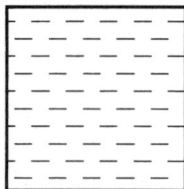

DASH

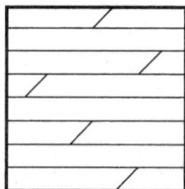

DOLMIT

DOTS

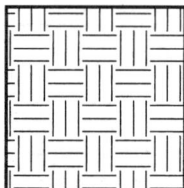

EARTH

ESCHER

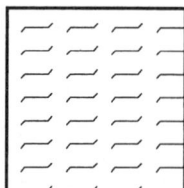

FLEX

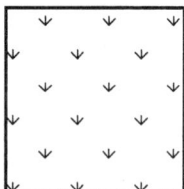

GRASS

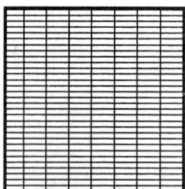

GRATE

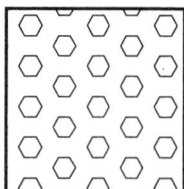

HEX

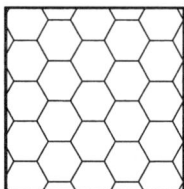

HONEY

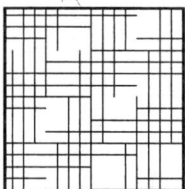

HOUND

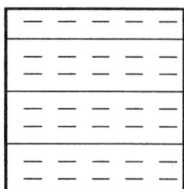

INSUL

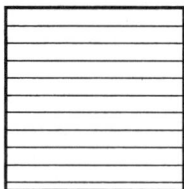

LINE

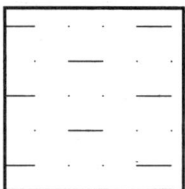

MUDST

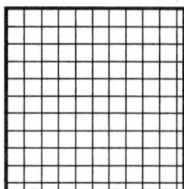

NET

NET3

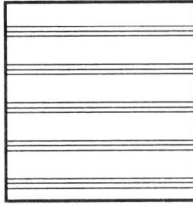

PLAST

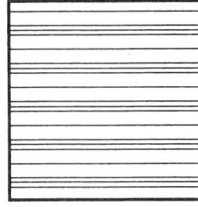

PLASTI

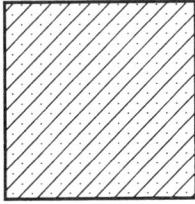

SACNCR

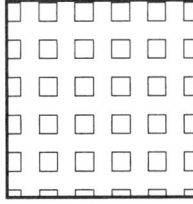

SQUARE

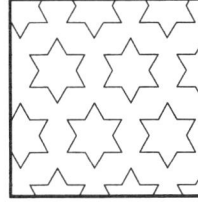

STARS

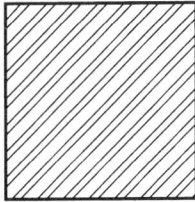

STEEL

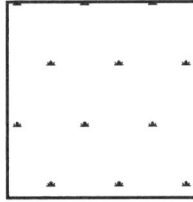

SWAMP

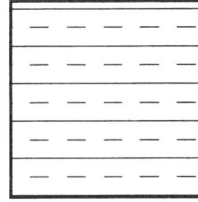

TRANS

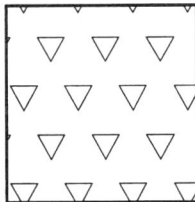

TRIANG

ZIGZAG

A list of linetype styles follows on p.150.

Linetype Styles

In addition to the Continuous linetype there are 24 linetype styles that can be loaded from *acltiso.lin:*

BORDER

BORDER2

BORDERX2

CENTER(& CENTER)

CENTER2

CENTERX2

DASHDOT

DASHDOT2

DASHDOTX2

DASHED

DASHED2

DASHEDX2

DIVIDE

DIVIDE2

DIVIDEX2

DOT

DOT2

DOTX2

HIDDEN

HIDDEN2

HIDDENX2

PHANTOM

PHANTOM2

PHANTOMX2

Index

Fillet 69, 112
FILLET 111, 136
Function keys 7

G

General information 128
GETENV 136
Getting started 1
Graphics Area 6
GRAPHSCR 136
GRID 41, 136
grips 91

H

HANDLES 136
Hardware and software 128
HATCH 74, 136
  list of patterns 146
HATCHEDIT 136
HELP 20, 136
  online 28
HIDE 137

I

ID 59, 137
INSERT 137
ISOPLANE 137

L

LAYER 42, 137
Layer 21, 143
  changing 103
  creating 31
  dialogue box 21
  name 21
Layer colour 21
  changing 31
Layer control 5
Layering drawings
  the concept of 30

Layers
  making invisible 73
LIMITS 42, 137
LINE 137
LINETYPE 137
  changing 32, 104
  list of styles 150
LIST 137
LTSCALE 137

M

MEASURE 138
MIRROR 60, 110, 138
Mirrtext
  system variable 110
Model Space *See also* Paper
    Space
  icon 87
  plotting from 89
Modify command 50
MOVE 97, 138
MS-DOS Windows 1
MSLIDE 138
MSPACE 4, 138
MULTIPLE 138
MVIEW 138

N

NEW 19, 138

O

Object Snap 54
  endpoint 58
  intersection 59
  midpoint 55
  nearest 62
  perpendicular 58
  quadrant 70
OFFSET 56, 138
OOPS 138

Software Licence

AUTODESK, INC. SOFTWARE LICENCE AGREEMENT

PLEASE READ THIS CAREFULLY. IT CONTAINS THE TERMS ON
WHICH THIS AUTODESK COMPUTER PROGRAM IS BEING
LICENSED TO YOU. IF YOU DO NOT AGREE TO THESE TERMS,
RETURN ALL THE ITEMS IN THIS PACKAGE TO YOUR SUPPLIER
FOR A FULL REFUND. IF YOU ARE OBTAINING AN
AUTHORISATION CODE TO ACCESS A COMPUTER PROGRAM
SUBJECT TO THE TERMS OF THIS LICENCE, OBTAINING AND
USING THE AUTHORISATION CODE TO ACCESS THE PROGRAM
WILL BE DEEMED TO BE YOUR CONSENT TO THE LICENCE
TERMS. NO REFUND WILL BE GRANTED ONCE THE
AUTHORISATION CODE HAS BEEN ISSUED.

COPYING OF THIS COMPUTER PROGRAM OR ITS
DOCUMENTATION EXCEPT AS PERMITTED BY THIS LICENCE IS
COPYRIGHT INFRINGEMENT UNDER THE LAWS OF YOUR
COUNTRY. IF YOU COPY THIS COMPUTER PROGRAM WITHOUT
PERMISSION OF AUTODESK, YOU ARE VIOLATING THE LAW. YOU
MAY BE LIABLE TO AUTODESK FOR DAMAGES, AND YOU MAY BE
SUBJECT TO CRIMINAL PENALTIES.

POSSESSION OR USE FOR COMMERCIAL PURPOSES OF ANY
PROGRAM, DEVICE OR OTHER MEANS INTENDED TO
FACILITATE REMOVAL OR CIRCUMVENTION OF ANY HARDWARE
LOCK OR NODE IDENTIFICATION NUMBER WITH WHICH THIS
COMPUTER PROGRAM IS SUPPLIED IS PROHIBITED.

1.   Grant of licence

In consideration of your agreement to the terms of this Agreement
Autodesk, Inc. ("Autodesk") grants you a nonexclusive, nontransferable
licence to use the enclosed computer program (the "Software") and its
accompanying documentation ("Documentation") on equipment owned
by you or under your control according to the terms and conditions
below. This Agreement permits a single user to use the Software on only
one computer at one location at any one time.

If this Software is an educational version, you may use it only for the
purpose of training and instruction and for no other purpose. If this

Software is a student version, it may be used only by the student who acquired it and only for study and instruction.

Regardless of which alternative you choose, this Agreement permits you to make only one backup copy of the Software. This Software Package may contain a printed manual and accompanying documentation (the "Documentation") or electronic Documentation. If the Documentation is in printed form, it may not be copied. If the Documentation is in electronic form, you may print out one (1) copy, which may not be copied.

2.   Restrictions

You may not:

a.   copy the Software or Documentation except as permitted by this Agreement.

b.   reverse engineer, decompile or disassemble the Software except that you may decompile the Software only to the extent permitted by law where this is indispensable to obtain the information necessary to achieve interoperability of an independently created program with the Software or with another program and such information is not readily available from Autodesk or elsewhere. You may not decompile the Software if such information is available by licensing any Autodesk Software Developer's Kit through an Authorized Autodesk Dealer or your local Autodesk office.

c.   distribute, rent, loan, sell, sublicense or otherwise transfer all or part of the Software, Documentation or any rights granted hereunder to any other person without the prior written consent of Autodesk.

d.   remove, alter or obscure any proprietary notices, labels or marks from the Software or Documentation.

e.   modify, translate, adapt or arrange the Software or Documentation, or create derivative works based on the Software or Documentation, for any purpose.

f.   utilize any equipment, device, software, information or other means designed or adapted to circumvent or remove any form of copy protection used by Autodesk in connection with the Software, or use the Software together with any hardware lock or other copy protection device not supplied by Autodesk or an Authorized Autodesk Dealer.

g.   If this is a workstation version of the Software it is supplied with a specific node identification number and is authorized for use only on the workstation or server carrying that identification number. You may not alter the node identification number in any manner or for any purpose so as to permit the Software to be used on any other workstation or server.

3.   Software Provided on More than One Medium

Except as provided below, if the Software is provided on more than one medium, you may use only one appropriate medium. You may not distribute, rent, loan, sell, sublicense or otherwise transfer the other medium or media except with the prior written consent of Autodesk or Autodesk Press.

If more than one operating system version of the Software is provided, you may use either or both, but only as permitted by Section 1 (Grant of Licence) above. As the sole exception to this provision, you may load and run a single session of a Microsoft® MS-DOS® version simultaneously with a single session of a Microsoft Windows™ version.

4.   Upgrades and Updates

If this Software is being licensed to you as an upgrade or update to software previously licensed to you, you must, if instructed by Autodesk Press or the local Autodesk office, destroy all copies of the software previously licensed to you, including any copies resident on your hard disk drive, and return to the local Autodesk office any hardware lock which accompanied the software previously licensed to you.

5.   Copyright

Ownership and copyrights in the AutoCAD LT Software and Documentation and any copies made by you remain with Autodesk & Autodesk Press. Ownership and copyrights in the Manual shall remain with Autodesk Press an ITP company.

Unauthorized copying of the Software or Documentation or failure to comply with any of the terms of this Agreement will result in automatic termination òf this Agreement. Any use of any copies of the Software or Documentation after termination of this agreement is unlawful.

6.   Warranty

Autodesk Press warrants that the Software will provide the facilities and functions generally described in the Documentation and that the media on which the Software is furnished, the Documentation accompanying the Software, and any hardware lock or other copy protection device accompanying the Software will be free from defects in materials and workmanship under normal use. Autodesk Press's entire liability and your exclusive remedy under these warranties will be, at Autodesk Press's option, to attempt to correct or work around errors, to replace the defective media, documentation or copy protection device, or to refund the licence fee and terminate this Agreement. This remedy is subject to the return of the defective media, documentation or copy protection device with a copy of your receipt to Autodesk Press or the supplier from whom it was obtained within ninety (90) days from the date of its delivery to you. Following expiration of this ninety (90)-day period, Autodesk Press will replace any defective or damaged copy protection device in return for payment of an amount which covers the cost of a replacement device plus a fee for handling and shipment.

EXCEPT FOR THE ABOVE EXPRESS LIMITED WARRANTIES, AUTODESK PRESS MAKES AND YOU RECEIVE NO WARRANTIES, EXPRESS, IMPLIED, STATUTORY OR IN ANY COMMUNICATION WITH YOU, AND AUTODESK PRESS SPECIFICALLY DISCLAIMS ANY OTHER WARRANTY INCLUDING THE IMPLIED WARRANTY OF MERCHANTABILITY OR FITNESS FOR A PARTICULAR PURPOSE. AUTODESK PRESS DOES NOT WARRANT THAT THE OPERATION OF THE SOFTWARE WILL BE UNINTERRUPTED OR ERROR FREE.

7.   Disclaimer

COMPUTER-AIDED DESIGN SOFTWARE AND OTHER TECHNICAL SOFTWARE ARE TOOLS INTENDED TO BE USED BY TRAINED PROFESSIONALS ONLY. THEY ARE NOT

SUBSTITUTES FOR YOUR PROFESSIONAL JUDGMENT.
COMPUTER-AIDED DESIGN SOFTWARE AND OTHER
TECHNICAL SOFTWARE ARE INTENDED TO ASSIST WITH
PRODUCT DESIGN AND ARE NOT SUBSTITUTES FOR
INDEPENDENT TESTING OF PRODUCT STRESS, SAFETY
AND UTILITY. DUE TO THE LARGE VARIETY OF POTENTIAL
APPLICATIONS FOR THE SOFTWARE, THE SOFTWARE HAS
NOT BEEN TESTED IN ALL SITUATIONS UNDER WHICH IT
MAY BE USED. NEITHER AUTODESK NOR AUTODESK PRESS
SHALL BE LIABLE IN ANY MANNER WHATSOEVER FOR
THE RESULTS OBTAINED THROUGH THE USE OF THE
SOFTWARE. PERSONS USING THE SOFTWARE ARE
RESPONSIBLE FOR THE SUPERVISION, MANAGEMENT AND
CONTROL OF THE SOFTWARE. THIS RESPONSIBILITY
INCLUDES THE DETERMINATION OF APPROPRIATE USES
FOR THE SOFTWARE AND THE SELECTION OF THE
SOFTWARE AND OTHER PROGRAMS TO ACHIEVE
INTENDED RESULTS. PERSONS USING THE SOFTWARE ARE
ALSO RESPONSIBLE FOR ESTABLISHING THE ADEQUACY
OF INDEPENDENT PROCEDURES FOR TESTING THE
RELIABILITY AND ACCURACY OF ANY PROGRAM OUTPUT,
INCLUDING ALL ITEMS DESIGNED BY USING THE
SOFTWARE.

8.   Limitation of Liability

IN NO EVENT WILL EITHER AUTODESK OR AUTODESK
PRESS BE LIABLE FOR ANY LOSS OR DAMAGE OF ANY
KIND, INCLUDING LOSS OF DATA, LOST PROFITS, COST OF
COVER OR OTHER SPECIAL, INCIDENTAL,
CONSEQUENTIAL OR INDIRECT DAMAGES ARISING OUT OF
THE USE OR INABILITY TO USE THE SOFTWARE OR
DOCUMENTATION, HOWEVER CAUSED AND ON ANY
THEORY OF LIABILITY INCLUDING UNDER CONTRACT,
NEGLIGENCE OR OTHERWISE. THIS LIMITATION WILL
APPLY EVEN IF AUTODESK, AUTODESK PRESS OR ANY
AUTODESK DEALER HAS BEEN ADVISED OF THE
POSSIBILITY OF SUCH LOSS OR DAMAGE. YOU
ACKNOWLEDGE THAT THE LICENCE FEE REFLECTS THIS
ALLOCATION OF RISK.

NEITHER AUTODESK NOT AUTODESK PRESS SHALL HAVE
ANY RESPONSIBILITY OR LIABILITY WHATSOEVER
ARISING FROM LOSS OR THEFT OF THE SOFTWARE OR OF
ANY COPY PROTECTION DEVICE WITH WHICH THE
SOFTWARE IS SUPPLIED. SPECIFICALLY, NEITHER
AUTODESK NOR AUTODESK PRESS SHALL BE OBLIGATED
TO REPLACE ANY LOST OR STOLEN SOFTWARE OR COPY
PROTECTION DEVICE. YOU ARE SOLELY RESPONSIBLE FOR
SAFEGUARDING THE SOFTWARE AND ANY COPY
PROTECTION DEVICE FROM LOSS OR THEFT AND
PROTECTING YOUR INVESTMENT THROUGH INSURANCE
OR OTHERWISE.

IN THE EVENT THAT ANY EXCLUSION, DISCLAIMER OR
OTHER PROVISIONS CONTAINED IN THIS AGREEMENT
SHALL BE HELD INVALID FOR ANY REASON AND
AUTODESK OR AUTODESK PRESS BECOMES LIABLE FOR
LOSS OR DAMAGE THAT COULD OTHERWISE HAVE BEEN
LIMITED, SUCH LIABILITY, WHETHER IN CONTRACT,
NEGLIGENCE OR OTHERWISE, SHALL NOT EXCEED £25,000.

AUTODESK DOES NOT EXCLUDE LIABILITY FOR DEATH OR
PERSONAL INJURY RESULTING FROM THE NEGLIGENCE OF
AUTODESK OR LIABILITY FOR DAMAGE CAUSED BY A
DEFECT IN THE SOFTWARE WITHIN THE MEANING OF PART
1 OF THE CONSUMER PROTECTION ACT 1987, TO WHICH NO
LIMIT APPLIES.

9. General

a. This Agreement shall terminate without further notice or action
by Autodesk if you become bankrupt, go into liquidation, suffer
or make any winding-up petition, make an arrangement with your
creditors, have an administrator, administrative receiver or receiver
appointed or suffer or take any similar action in consequence of
debt.

b. This Agreement shall not be governed by the 1980 Convention
on Contracts for the Sale of Goods but by the laws of England and
shall be subject to the jurisdiction of the English Courts. This

Agreement is the entire agreement between us and supersedes any other communications, representations, or advertising with respect to the Software and Documentation. If you have any questions, please contact your supplier.

If any part of this Agreement is held by a court of competent jurisdiction to be unenforceable, the validity of the remainder of the Agreement shall not be affected.

Nothing herein shall affect the statutory rights of consumers in "consumer transactions" under any applicable legislation.

You agree that Autodesk takes the benefit of the provisions of this Agreement for itself and as agent for any other entity from time to time forming part of the Autodesk group.

Autodesk and the Autodesk logo are registered trademarks of Autodesk, Inc. in the United States of America and other countries. All other brand names, product names, or trademarks belong to their respective holders.